P9-DFM-316

# AT THE
# THRESHOLD
## OF THE
# MILLENNIUM

Edited by
Donovan R. Walling

Phi Delta Kappa
Educational Foundation
Bloomington, Indiana

Cover design by
Peg Caudell

Library of Congress Catalog Number 95-69266
ISBN 0-87367-481-2 (pbk.)
Copyright © 1995 by the Phi Delta Kappa Educational Foundation
Bloomington, Indiana

This book is sponsored by Bessie Gabbard, chair of the Board of Governors of the Phi Delta Kappa Educational Foundation and a member of the Ohio State University and Broward County Florida Chapters of Phi Delta Kappa, who made a generous contribution toward publication costs. Miss Gabbard was the first woman to be initiated to membership in PDK.

# PUBLISHED IN HONOR OF

Lowell C. Rose
Phi Delta Kappa Executive Director
1971-1995

Lowell C. Rose began his service as executive director of Phi Delta Kappa on 1 September 1971, becoming only the third executive director in the fraternity's history. His retirement in 1995 marks the end of a remarkable 24-year tenure.

When Lowell Rose became executive director, PDK boasted 85,000 members in 380 chapters. Now, nearly a quarter-century later, the fraternity has grown to some 130,000 members in nearly 700 chapters, with chapters in Canada, the Virgin Islands, Guam, the United Kingdom, Germany, Korea, Belgium, Italy, Thailand, Okinawa, the Philippines, Japan, Taiwan, Spain, and Bermuda, in addition to those in the United States.

Along with substantial membership growth, Dr. Rose has overseen major program growth, particularly in program dissemination and professional development. Major additions have been made to the Bloomington, Indiana, headquarters building, including the construction of the International Conference Center, where PDK plays host each summer to hundreds of educators from across the country and abroad who come to Bloomington to participate in the Gabbard Institutes, a series of professional seminars.

Shortly after assuming his duties as executive director of PDK, Dr. Rose also supervised a major change in the membership: the admission of women to the fraternity. This change in 1974 can be felt today, as evidenced by the many women in leadership positions at the chapter and district levels. Indeed, the fraternity's membership now is nearly 60% women.

Lowell Rose is a graduate of Rushville (Indiana) High School; Ball State University in Muncie, Indiana; and Purdue University. He has received Distinguished Alumnus Awards from both Ball State and Purdue. He holds a B.S. degree in social studies and business education, an M.A. in social studies, and a Ph.D. in school administration.

Dr. Rose began his career in education as a secondary school social studies teacher in DeMotte and Griffith, Indiana. While completing his doctorate at Purdue University, he worked as a part-time instructor there and as director of the School Survey Team, studying the needs of schools in the Lafayette, Indiana, area townships.

After completing his doctoral work, Dr. Rose returned to the public schools as a social studies teacher at North Central High School in Washington Township in suburban Indianapolis and, later, as director of research, information, and testing for the Washington Township school district. During this period, he also worked as a summer lecturer in school administration, research, and personnel relations at Butler University in Indianapolis.

In 1963, Dr. Rose was appointed as assistant superintendent of the Kokomo-Center Township Consolidated School Corporation north of Indianapolis. One year later, at the age of 37, he was appointed as superintendent of those schools, a position he held until 1967. Under his leadership, Kokomo established its first public school kindergartens and constructed a second high school.

Dr. Rose moved to Bloomington in 1967 to accept the positions of executive secretary for the Indiana School Boards Association and associate professor of education at Indiana University. From 1967 until 1971, he taught graduate classes in school law, coordinated the statewide activities of the ISBA-member school boards, and served as editor of the association's journal. His duties also included working with state legislators, school boards, and superintendents in writing legislation and providing assistance with research, orientation, and legal services.

The appointment in 1971 of Lowell Rose to the position of PDK Executive Secretary (as it was then titled) marked the culmination of several years of service to PDK up to that time. Dr. Rose had been initiated into PDK in 1958. He had served as the area coordinator for Indiana from 1966 until 1968; and from 1968 until his appointment as chief administrative officer for the fraternity, he was the District V Representative.

When Dr. Rose announced his retirement, he was quoted in the fraternity newsletter, *News, Notes, and Quotes*:

I have been most pleased that we have been able, during my time with Phi Delta Kappa, to move the organization from one that was primarily social and fraternal to one that has an important professional mission. We have surrounded the *Phi Delta Kappan* with significant programs in research, dissemination, and professional development.

Professional development, in particular, has been a mark of achievement in Dr. Rose's tenure with PDK. And the Phi Delta Kappa Educational Foundation was particularly influential in that program expansion during the 1970s and 1980s. Between 1971 and 1989, PDK instituted a number of programs that continue to grow and to benefit members and nonmember educators alike. Much credit for this growth must be given to Dr. Rose and the chair of the Foundation Board of Governors, Bessie Gabbard.

Among the achievements of the Foundation are the fastback series of authoritative, readable, short publications; the Reavis Reading Area collections of materials in schools and libraries literally around the world; the author seminar program that sends authors to PDK chapters everywhere; and a wealth of scholarship opportunites, among them the prospective educator scholarships, the Gerald Read International Travel Seminar scholarships, the Howard M. Soule Graduate Fellowships, and the Victoria C.T. Read Adopt-a-Scholar program.

Dr. Rose also has been instrumental in forging collaborative arrangements with other professional organizations. PDK's leadership of Future Educators of America is a noteworthy example. Most recently, PDK's close ties with the Institute for Educational Leadership has led to co-sponsorship with IEL of the Center on National Education Policy, which provides for the first time a Washington, D.C., presence for Phi Delta Kappa.

Recently, Lowell and his wife, Mary, ensured that their personal influence would be felt long after retirement through the generous gift of $10,000 to the PDK Educational Foundation. The Lowell C. and Mary J. Rose Endowed Scholarship Fund will provide PDK's first renewable scholarships for prospective educators. The $10,000 initial endowment already has been more than doubled by generous gifts from PDK's extended family of members, and the endowment continues to grow.

In nearly a quarter-century of leadership, Lowell Rose not only has promoted the growth of the fraternity and enlarged its facilities and services, he also has enhanced PDK's influence on education both nationally and internationally. The lasting contributions of Lowell Rose to Phi

Delta Kappa set the stage for a future that will be positive and productive. Dr. Rose's leadership has ensured that PDK will play a signficant role in shaping American education in the years to come.

Sandra Weith
Director of the Administrative Center
Phi Delta Kappa International Headquarters

# TABLE OF CONTENTS

**Introduction** .......................................... 1

**Believing in Education and Facing the Challenges of the 1990s**
by John F. Jennings .............................. 3

**At the Threshold of the Millennium**
by Bessie Gabbard .............................. 7

**Education for the 21st Century**
by Michael D. Usdan .......................... 13

**The Chameleon's Dish, Promise-Crammed**
by Stanley Elam .............................. 23

**Civic Disengagement and the Attack on Public Education**
by Donovan R. Walling .......................... 33

**Professionals and Politics**
by Jack Frymier .............................. 43

**Education — Past, Present, Future**
by George M. Thomas .......................... 51

**Help Wanted: Educational Entrepreneurs**
by Donald P. Anderson .......................... 57

**Enhancing the Presence of African-American Teachers**
by Howard D. Hill .............................. 65

**Can Educators Give Up Control of Learning?**
by Douglas Bedient .......................... 77

**The Struggle for the Survival of the Common School**
by David L. Clark .............................. 81

**Reflections of an Urban Educator**
by Jack Kosoy . . . . . . . . . . . . . . . . . . . . . . . . . . . . . . . . .   89

**For the Love of Learning**
by Arliss L. Roaden . . . . . . . . . . . . . . . . . . . . . . . . . . . . .   95

**An Eye on the Future in South Africa**
by Neville Robertson . . . . . . . . . . . . . . . . . . . . . . . . . . . . .  103

# INTRODUCTION

How should an organization appropriately recognize and honor the accomplishments of its retiring leader? That question was posed by the Board of Governors of the Phi Delta Kappa Educational Foundation in response to the announcement that Lowell C. Rose, who had served Phi Delta Kappa as its executive director for nearly a quarter-century, would retire in 1995.

As might be supposed, the responses to that question were many and varied. One idea that rose above the rest has now been realized in this volume of essays. *At the Threshold of the Millennium* is a tribute both to the ideals of Phi Delta Kappa and to the inquiring spirit of Lowell C. Rose.

In my invitation to the writers in this volume to contribute an essay, I asked each person not for a direct tribute to Lowell Rose, but rather for an "essay" in the truest sense of that word. I sought a "trial of the value or nature" of an idea that represented "a personal view of the author." I invited each writer to reflect on his or her experiences in education and in life, to draw from that well of personal history, and then to look ahead — to cross the threshold of the millennium by speculating on what education in the 21st century might, should, and can be. By so doing, I hoped that these essays would mirror the Phi Delta Kappa ideals of research, service, and leadership, to which Dr. Rose has dedicated his 24 years of leadership in PDK.

The responses do not disappoint. The writers, most of them senior educators with great depth and breadth of experience, bring into focus their own special stories and concerns. Their stories are as diverse as they are themselves. But, moreover, the essays spring forward from those varied histories to look into the future, offering concerned, sometimes impassioned perspectives and urging specific directions that the writers believe will improve education for students in the next century.

1

A broad range of topics is addressed, from *Kappan* editor emeritus Stan Elam's reflective "The Chameleon's Dish, Promise-Crammed" and Bessie Gabbard's ninety-year perspective in the title essay to contemporary issues, such as the recruitment and retention of African-American educators in Howard Hill's "Enhancing the Presence of African-American Teachers" and Don Anderson's look at innovation and motivation in his "Help Wanted: Educational Entrepreneurs."

*At the Threshold of the Millennium* announces no specific, unifying theme. Rather, the essays are intended — from perspectives as diverse as the issues confronting American education — to stand at the threshold. The authors are in the doorway of the 21st century, glancing back over their many experiences in the past and then turning to look forward, attempting to see the future. The writing challenge was both daunting and engaging. Responding to my invitation, Bessie Gabbard wrote, "This is a big ORDER. I shall do my best." Indeed, that is precisely what she and the other writers did.

As a result, readers will find in this volume reflections and reminiscences that tug at familiar corners of memory, ideas and issues that raise important questions, and suggestions and recommendations that merit serious contemplation. In this spirit, these essays compose a fitting tribute to the man who, as Phi Delta Kappa's executive director since 1971, has challenged the professional fraternity to look both inward and outward in order to provide — not merely for today, but also for the future — a voice of mature, thoughtful leadership in American education. On the occasion of his retirement, this book honors Lowell C. Rose.

# BELIEVING IN EDUCATION
# AND FACING THE
# CHALLENGES OF THE 1990s

by John F. Jennings

*John F. (Jack) Jennings is director of the Center on National Educa-tion Policy in Washington, D.C. The Center is co-sponsored by Phi Delta Kappa and the Institute for Educational Leadership. Jack, former general counsel for education, Committee on Education and Labor, U.S. House of Representatives, developed and edited the recent Nation-al Issues in Education series of PDK/IEL books. That four-volume series offers an in-depth view of the education legislation of the Clinton Administration.*

The American public shares a bedrock belief in education. At the beginning of the republic Thomas Jefferson spoke of an educated citi-zenry as essential to democracy. A century and a half later James Bryant Conant said: "The primary concern of American education today . . . is to cultivate in the largest possible number of our future citizens an appreciation of both the responsibilities and the benefits which come to them because they are Americans and are free." Throughout American history we have valued education and considered expanding education-al opportunities to more and more citizens as important to our very existence as a country.

The task before us today is to try to understand how a core belief in public education can survive in this new age, when the world seems to be coming together and falling apart at the same time. Through the wonders of modern telecommunications, it seems that everyone knows everything about every part of the globe. We are coming together in a global sense through our common awareness of events. Yet, simultane-ously, we are growing apart in other ways. As neighbors, we know less of one another with every successive generation, and our neighbor-hoods seem to become more dangerous.

In the 1950s and early 1960s, when I was in elementary and secondary schools, our society was different from today's society. Students were more disciplined. More mothers were at home and not in the job market, and so they supervised their children after school and often made them do their homework. And there was much less television.

Today, in the society of the 1990s, most families have both parents working outside the home, even if they have young children who are not yet in school. Therefore, many more children do not have parental supervision after school. Additionally, more teenagers have jobs after school in order to earn spending money. And there is much more television viewing.

The *Washington Post* of 10 April 1995 wrote of these changes over the past four decades: "There's been a change in children's behavior in the past few years and it's not for the better." Numerous reports have reached that conclusion, based on the observations of teachers, principals, and researchers.

The *Post* reported that teachers are seeing more children who have a hard time understanding limits and dealing with frustrations. These children want everything their own way and cannot wait their turn. According to the newspaper article, teachers claim that some of this lack of connectedness can be traced to parents spending less time with their children, most probably because they are spending more time on their job.

Another factor is that many parents feel guilty about being away from their family because of work, and so they try to offer their children a "worry-free" environment. The children have all the freedom and amenities they want. Again according to the article, teachers say that treating children this way at home results in the children being unable to deal with frustrations or to work things out themselves and to respect others.

These findings are important because they resonate with so much that teachers have said over the last few years. Children are coming to school with less productive attitudes, and those attitudes are negatively affecting classroom behavior. Of course, this is not true of all children; but the repetition of these complaints from teachers and principals means that the change is noteworthy.

The irony is that American parents today think that education is even more important to the welfare of their children than in the past. In fact, they urge their children in increasing numbers to pursue schooling through college, because they see that those with more education are the ones who are better able to survive in the job market in these turbulent times. According to the National Center for Education Statistics, parents of all ethnic groups and of every income level are counseling their children to continue their schooling and to go to college.

But giving advice to continue in school is not what matters the most in determining whether a child is able to obtain a good education. Rather, the self-discipline and the social attitudes that a child learns at home are vitally important. In speaking of higher education in Scotland in the 1920s, James Barrie said: "Mighty are the Universities of Scotland, and they will prevail. But even in your highest exultations never forget that they are not four, but five. The greatest of them is the poor, proud homes you come out of, which said so long ago: 'There shall be education in this land.'" In other words, the home is perhaps the greatest school of all in shaping a child's character and attitudes toward life.

In researching the reasons that there were differences in the attainment of mathematics skills among children participating in the National Assessment of Educational Progress, the Educational Testing Service found that the five most significant factors involved the home environment of children. These factors included the number of days that a student was absent from school, the number of hours a student spent watching television, the number of pages read for homework, the quantity and type of reading material in the home, and the presence of two parents in the house. ETS estimated that these five factors accounted for 91% of the differences among the states in average proficiency attained by students.

The United States is now in its second decade of substantial school reform, probably the longest period that we as a nation have concentrated on trying to improve the schools. This reform must go further than it has and must become deeply imbedded in every school. But changing the institution of school can go only so far. Real gains in achievement may not be achieved until the culture of the modern American home also is reformed.

Our collective bedrock belief in public education will survive because it is so much a part of our character as a people. But in the middle of the 1990s we have to broaden our view of education to renew our understanding that home and family are the first and most important school. The attitudes and values taught there must be sound if a child is to benefit from public education.

# AT THE THRESHOLD OF
# THE MILLENNIUM

## by Bessie Gabbard

*Bessie Gabbard, fondly regarded as the "First Lady of PDK," chairs the Phi Delta Kappa Educational Foundation Board of Governors. She became the first woman admitted to PDK when the formerly all-male fraternity welcomed women members for the first time in 1974, but her association with PDK began nearly a decade earlier with the establishment of the Educational Foundation by her friend and colleague George Reavis. Bessie began her career as a kindergarten teacher and later became the host of a national radio program for children sponsored by the Ohio Department of Education. As the radio "Story Lady," she delighted young listeners with her spirited readings of children's tales, including more than 500 that she wrote herself.*

Change is inevitable. And change is good. When some changes do not satisfy us, we start over — and change again.

The drastic changes affecting education in the latter part of the 20th century will be reflected in our society and its schools in the 21st century. Public schools have become a routine target for national criticism. Daily, the media portray the problems of public schools. Critics urge schools to take more leadership in the fight against teenage pregnancy and the use of drugs and the spread crime, in the prevention of youth suicide and the spread of AIDS. Today's schools are expected to take responsibility for what previous generations considered to be the duties of the family. And as the 21st century opens, the public schools will continue to be charged with meeting not merely the academic needs of students, but their basic needs for nurture, nutrition, and health care.

These are daunting responsibilities. Somehow, we must reinvigorate community spirit and personal accountability. I believe that every citizen in every community should be concerned about and take responsibility for the schools we want for our children — and for the children themselves.

I was born in 1905. In my ninety years, I have witnessed many educational, social, and economic changes. At the age of four, I experienced my first ride in an automobile. Our family doctor had just purchased a new Maxwell open-air automobile and gave my mother and me a ride. My mother had to wear a duster (a scarf) to protect her hairdo from the wind and dust.

The Air Age had been launched at the time of my birth. Thirty years later, I learned to fly a Cessna. While serving as an elementary principal at the edge of a large airport, I realized that we were in a learning center where the students, from kindergartners to eighth-graders, could study the great invention of the Wright brothers.

During my high school days in the 1920s, I recall the excitement of taking my turn, with the family, to put on earphones and listen to the nightly radio news. There were sputtering noises to be endured, and the news was mostly local.

My four-year-old brother, who enjoyed watching the activities in the street more than listening to the radio, had the duty of placing the ice-card in the window. The card told the ice man how many pounds of ice our family needed in those days before electric refrigerators. He also tried to imitate the shrill call of the umbrella man who walked down the sidewalk calling, "UM-BRRREL-LAS to mend!"

By the early 1930s, radio was a standard feature of most homes. And I was privileged to use it to enrich the classroom experience of children as "The Story Lady," a role I played one day a week for more than ten years. The reading program was part of the School of the Air, sponsored by the Ohio State Department of Education and broadcast over WLW in Cincinnati, Ohio. Later, I helped develop television programs for the Cincinnati Public Schools on WCET.

The 20th century has introduced a wealth of telecommunications and technology for the home and the classroom. With the use of televisions and computers, textbooks and atlases are becoming obsolete. The pace for learning has been accelerated. Students today are seeing history in the making, and the effects of technology will shape much of schooling and learning in the 21st Century.

But the changes go beyond technology, too. The one-room country school at the beginning of this century was vastly different from our large, complex schools today. My maternal grandmother, Kathryn, was a teacher, principal, and superintendent in a one-room country school. Everyone in the county knew and respected her. She was the mother of ten children. The eldest daughter, my mother, cared for the children who were not in school. Grandmother Kathryn kept her most recent baby in a cradle beside her desk. She nursed this infant during recess periods. She tended the wood-burning stove herself and assigned older students to see that the drinking-water bucket was filled. A single gourd dipper was used by all the students.

Today, at the approach of the 21st century, it is not unusual to see grandparents caring for their grandchildren. The family structure has changed. To keep up with social and economic changes, it has become necessary for not one parent but both parents to work. Today, children with divorced parents are a majority in many schools. A startling number of unmarried teenagers have children. The breakdown of the traditional family accounts for many of the problems in today's society.

Particularly during the past quarter-century, educators have witnessed rapid economic, social, and demographic changes that affect families. And educators must recognize and deal positively with these changes. Stephanie Coontz, in a *Kappan* special report for March 1995, "The American Family and the Nostalgia Trap," concludes with these words: "We have to adjust our economic programs, schools, work policies, ex-pectations of family life, and moral reasoning to the realities of family diversity and the challenges of global transformation."

Contrast the public school problems found in the Gallup Poll of 1994 with some of the problems in the early 1900s. I can still remem-ber some of the problems my fifth-grade teacher faced: throwing paper wads (or spit balls), chewing gum, getting out of line, and talking out of turn. We once received a free day out of school because some boys placed Limburger cheese on a hot radiator. The schools had to be aired before we could re-enter. The 26th Annual Phi Delta Kappa/Gallup Poll of the Public's Attitudes Toward the Public Schools, by Stanley M. Elam, Lowell C. Rose, and Alec Gallup, in the *Kappan* for September 1994, lists two problems as the most serious facing U.S. public schools today: 1) the growth of fighting/violence/gangs and 2) poor discipline.

Use of drugs, unwanted pregnancy, suicide, rape, robbery, and car-rying weapons are all problems that today's schools must face that the schools of the past rarely, if ever, encountered. From time to time, the government spends money to help schools counter these problems, but money alone is not the answer. Finding a lasting solution is going to take firm, united action by citizens in every community. We need to think collaboratively; to involve religious and social agencies, legisla-tors, and dedicated educators; and to take collective responsibility for changing the social climate.

For example, teacher empowerment is gaining acceptance, in spite of conflicting views, and collective bargaining continues to be effective in shaping district policies. In the past, teachers were limited mainly to the selection of textbooks or serving on advisory groups. Today, participatory decision making is a key element in the restructuring efforts of many school systems. Effective school management and positive labor relations require teamwork. For example, when the teachers in New Albany, Indiana, were frustrated and on the point of striking, the opposing sides brought in a facilitator. Through consensus bargaining, the teachers gained control of their school district's instructional budget. In this instance, these teachers took a risk. Leadership was crucial on both sides. Training — lots of it — was important. But the New Albany schools were committed to making a change, and it worked. Bargaining sessions became problem-solving sessions.

* * *

As I review my professional life, I see a trend to return to some of the educational philosophy of the past. The ideas of John Dewey, once misinterpreted and often criticized, are again being approved. Could it be that those who attack the public schools perform a public service by calling attention to shortcomings that can be addressed?

A great educator of the 20th century, Ralph Tyler, believed that the American public school was begun to educate the nation's children to assume the responsibility of citizenship in a democracy. Current polls and other evidence of present-day violence and crime indicate a lack of instruction by parents and schools to help students understand what it means to be a responsible citizen.

Thomas Jefferson wrote:

> I know of no safe depository of the ultimate powers of society but the people themselves; and if we think they are not enlightened enough to exercise their control with a wholesome discretion, the remedy is not to take it from them but to inform their discretion by education.

We Americans have invented the world's premiere system of universal free public education. Great efforts have been made to perfect this system. And there is no doubt our schools today differ from the traditional schools of the early 1900s. John I. Goodlad, writing in the 1994 second edition of his book, *What Schools Are For*, believes that it is time for all of us to join in the renewal of the common school.

At the same time, we do not agree on the course of that renewal. We divide on the use of vouchers and the choice of schools. Our Congress must face the problems of social legislation involving such divisive issues as gun control, prayer, and abortion.

10

Widespread involvement and interaction are needed between students, parents, teachers, administrators, community leaders, legislators, and religious groups to bring about reform for the common good. Local, state, and national legislative provisions must contribute to education reform. And with the changing dynamics of contemporary families, additional attention should be directed to the needs of children *before* they enter school.

Over the past 200 years one basic axiom has held our nation together. We, the people in a democracy, rule. We, the people in education, need to be cautious about where we place authority for influencing the education policies and practices of our schools. Gradually, we are turning to national (not federal), state, and local controls. Parents, teachers, and students are being empowered. There is an effort to create national voluntary support for educational changes through the establishment of high standards of academic content and occupational skills.

Dysfunctional families play a role in the decline of our society. Churches, social institutions, and education leaders have almost ignored the need to teach moral character. At the present time, many youth believe that whatever works is right — because it works. Thus, we must give attention to teaching ethical values in early childhood and reinforcing them throughout life.

Some religious leaders are critical that our nation is becoming more secular. Our forefathers built our nation on religious beliefs that are fundamental to our society. Our values and principles grow out of a Judeo-Christian tradition. All Americans must share responsibility for holding firm to this tradition, respecting our heritage, and prohibiting any restriction to the free exercise of religion.

As I write about changes in education over the past century and consider potential changes for the coming century, I hearken to my early experiences as a kindergarten teacher. Drastic changes have taken place in our society since 1900. But I continue to believe that the family is our first and best teacher. In early childhood, habits, attitudes, and values are learned that are essential to our future lives. And from these early foundations are built our future leaders.

In closing, I reflect on the leaders who have influenced my teaching, learning, and thinking. My mentors have been generous with their advice and wisdom. Two in particular stand out: George H. Reavis and Lowell C. Rose.

The vision and gifts of Dr. George H. Reavis made possible the establishment of the Phi Delta Kappa Educational Foundation. Dr. Reavis, assistant superintendent of the Cincinnati Public Schools and the director of a complete revision of the curriculum for the entire school system, served as my mentor from 1942 until his death in 1970. Dr. Reavis aroused my interest in the foundation and enabled me to be involved in its development. He designed the foundation to contribute to a better understanding of the educative process and the relation of education to human values.

Dr. Lowell C. Rose has served, effectively and formidably, for nearly a quarter-century as the executive director of Phi Delta Kappa. My professional association with Dr. Rose developed through serving as the chair of the Phi Delta Kappa Educational Foundation's Board of Governors. Dr. Rose, as a mentor, has been influential in helping me keep abreast of the issues that relate to quality education. His keen thinking and understanding of educational goals and standards have most recently led to the establishment, in cooperation with the Institute for Educational Leadership, of the Center on National Education Policy in Washington, D.C.

Phi Delta Kappa's connection with this center ensures an expanded partnership with states and local districts, where the actual work of education takes place.

# EDUCATION FOR THE 21st CENTURY

by Michael D. Usdan

*Michael D. Usdan is president of the Institute for Educational Leadership in Washington, D.C. IEL is a non-partisan institute whose mission is to support policies, programs, and practices that encourage leaders and their institutions to work together to improve educational opportunities and results for the nation's children and youth.*

I write from the perspective of an individual who is concerned about the whole panoply of social, economic, and political issues that so profoundly influence elementary and secondary education. I write as a generalist who believes that one of education's major problems is its traditional separation and isolation from other institutions in our society.

My contention is that education in the future will not be defined only in the conventional school or formal institutional context, but also as incorporating other deliverers of education or training services, such as the private sector, the military, voluntary associations, and the countless other organizations and agencies that provide education and training services. In other words, education will be defined as more than just traditional schooling. Outcome measures of student performance will continue to be stressed, and significant nonschool-centered social and economic factors will be employed in efforts to explain student achievement. Definitions of students and analyses of the learning process will be broadened to include recipients of educational services in a whole range of nonschool settings.

As the recent national reform movement reflects, political and business leaders, as well as the general public, will be willing to support increased funding for schools only if they are convinced that those dollars are generating positive results. This political fact of life augers an era of intensified accountability, in which schools in the increasingly competitive struggle for resources will have to justify their utility to a much greater extent on a cost-benefit basis. Unless the current weaknesses of education data and statistics are remedied and existing inadequacies and inaccuracies ameliorated, increased expenditures will not be politically viable. The necessary fiscal support will not be forthcoming in an aging nation in which fewer than 25% of adults have their own children enrolled in elementary and secondary schools.

The reform movement and the heightened interest of governors, civic elites, and influential business leaders will not last indefinitely and certainly will not be sustained without information that indicates which reforms work and which do not. Resources will not be available to support all of the multiple education reforms being enacted in states across the country. A priority for the future will be the development of better indicators that can help definitively determine the elements that strengthen student achievement.

A larger societal context in which elementary and secondary education issues will play out in the 21st century also must be considered. Broad human capital and adult learning issues — as well as conventional school matters — will have to be addressed in more connected ways in a changing and increasingly interdependent social, political and economic environment. American education is, in the redoubtable philosopher Pogo's words, "surrounded by insurmountable opportunities."

The recent attention that has been focused on schools by influential political and business leaders provides a unique opportunity for educators to broaden their base of political and economic support. Governors, state legislators, corporate executives, and the citizenry at large have recognized their collective stake in improving the quality of education if our nation is to compete in an increasingly technological and competitive international economy.

Like many other issues that periodically surface in American education, the need for close working relationships between the schools and business community is hardly new. Yet the need to build and sustain education-business collaboration becomes even more important as the American economy continues to be transformed in the Information Age. As technology changes rapidly and information burgeons, schools must interact with the private sector if young people and adults are to acquire essential skills.

The private sector has research and development capacities that simply are not present in either local or state education organizations or in the public sector generally. By the time equipment is procured in the public sector, it frequently is obsolete. Thus new arrangements must be developed so that students have access to state-of-the-art technology that currently is not available in most schools. Indeed, a persuasive case can be made that our society's economic viability may be predicated on sustaining and institutionalizing the current interest in business-education collaboration.

The economic problems facing our society call for unprecedented collaborations in every phase of American life. No longer is our economic growth unbridled and our products unchallenged in world markets, as our major manufacturing industries have discovered. We can no longer afford to be as unconcerned as we have been with productivity or quality standards. Educators at all levels in traditional institutions must acknowledge that they can no longer be isolated from other providers of education or training services, wherever those services are based — in the military, the private sector, community organizations, or elsewhere.

Schools have been discussed in the new and broader context of their central role in the collaborative efforts that will be necessary if the nation's economic productivity is to be improved and the erosion of its international competitive position arrested. Schools will remain pivotal to these national concerns, as awareness grows that education is the key to maximizing the nation's human capital and economic development. Support for educational improvement in the business community, for example, increasingly is viewed not as mere philanthropy but as essential to the self-interest of the private sector. Society's need to develop its human capital requires that education be defined as consisting of much more than formal elementary and secondary schools or colleges serving only the younger segment of the population.

Indeed, there is growing acceptance that human resources are the dominant factor in national income growth and that they account for the major share of the nation's total economic output. Current economic challenges are as fundamental as the change from an agrarian to an industrial economy after the Civil War, and education is linked inextricably to economic development and must be viewed as an essential investment in the future.

Schools in the 21st century must respond to new realities. If they do not, the private sector surely will react. The challenge educationally is not only to improve basic skills but also to react to the changes in occupational context that will compel more workers to shift from "take/place/lift/put" jobs to such work as computer programming that requires listening and reasoning skills, as well as a background in math and science. This challenge cannot be met by a single-sector approach.

15

As a society, we can no longer afford the luxury of "turfs." Meeting the challenge will require institutional collaborations among education, business, labor, and government. For example, many corporations allocate from 10% to 20% of the time of their engineers and other highly skilled personnel for inservice training so that they can keep abreast of rapid technological change. (Today's engineering graduate's experience will be relevant for five years, at best.) Organized labor also is acutely aware of the continuing need to re-educate and retrain its members. Recent labor contracts provide specific funds — per hour per employee — for training or educational activities. The education profession itself also must invest more in staff development.

## Some Salient Issues

Following is a brief — certainly not exhaustive or comprehensive — summary of the more salient issues that will confront education in the next century.

*Changes in the Nation's Demography.* Demographic data are important to the entire society, as well as to the schools. In a world in which more than 75% of the total population are persons of color, the United States must redefine *majority* and *minority*. About one-third of our public school population is of minority origin; and the proportion of blacks, Hispanics, Asian-Americans, and Native Americans continues to grow. In the public schools of the two largest states, California and Texas, minority children are, or nearly are, a majority. In other high-population states, such as New York, Florida, Illinois, and New Jersey, the minority school population represents a third or more of the enrollment. Twenty-three of our 25 largest school systems already are "majority minority." Unless we improve the quality of the education and the life chances of these massive cohorts of minority youngsters, our society may well be imperiled in the 21st century.

The Hispanic population is the fastest growing segment of the minority population, although approximately two-thirds of the nation's Hispanics live in only three states, California, Texas, and New York. In fact, more than 85% of the Hispanic population lives in only nine states — the previous three, New Jersey, Florida, Colorado, Illinois, New Mexico, and Arizona. This dramatic distribution skew creates a serious problem of demographic illiteracy, as the particular education needs of Hispanic children continue to be ignored in many schools.

The demographic phenomenon of "gray power" also will be increasingly significant as the population ages and the number of citizens 65

16

years of age or older rapidly increases. In 1990, the number of youngsters under 20 fell below 30% of the nation's population for the first time in history. Since 1983, there have been more people 65 years of age or older than teenagers. The implications of this trend can be seen in the ratio of working to retired people. In 1940, 10 citizens worked for every retired person; in 1985, the ratio was 5.3 to 1. By the year 2000, the ratio is predicted to be 4.7 to 1. And by 2030, a 2.7 to 1 ratio of workers to retired persons is considered possible.

Growing numbers of retired individuals will be dependent on a smaller, increasingly minority, population to sustain the economy and to maintain the viability of an already imperiled social security system. This "self-interest" argument is perhaps the most persuasive way of convincing an aging population that it has a direct interest in providing all youngsters with a quality education.

Such demographics illustrate why educators in the next century will have to broaden their base of political support. Education leaders no longer can assume the public support they could generate when, for example, 60% or 70% of the population had children in schools during the post-World War II era of rapid population growth. Today's schools and tomorrow's schools must cultivate new and broader constituencies if they are to acquire necessary support, as older citizens and other groups make increased demands for services in a period of declining public resources. Public schools will have to be viewed as a civic responsibility by the majority of the population, which will not have a direct stake in education.

*Recruiting and Retraining Quality Teachers.* A dominant theme in the recent education reform initiatives is the necessity of a high-quality teaching force. Without the requisite talent in the classroom, educational improvement will not occur. There is consensus that any effort to strengthen education and the development of our human capital must be predicated on improving the status and intellectual caliber of the classroom teachers who are at the core of education. In recent years, with the constraints on governmental spending, there has been a drain of talent from the public sector and service fields in general. Teaching is not attracting adequate numbers of our "best and brightest" young people, and more vigorous attempts must be made to replenish and strengthen the ranks of those responsible for developing the future intellectual capital that is so vital to our national security and well-being.

The problem is most acute in areas such as math and science, where the economic and status rewards of teaching cannot compare with the salaries and recognition available to talented individuals in businesses and industry. We have recognized that we have a crisis of national proportion because only about one-half of our math and science teachers are appropriately certified. Special initiatives to attract and retain math and science teachers — albeit controversial and politically volatile — must be considered.

The quality issue has been exacerbated by the fact that women, who constitute nearly two-thirds of the nation's classroom teachers, now have expanded career options, as do talented minorities. Intellectually able women and minorities who in the past entered teaching because other options were limited are now entering other professional fields. While this trend represents desirable and long-overdue social progress, it negatively affects the quality of the nation's teaching force. In particular, the percentage of minority teachers is declining at a time when the minority student population is rapidly increasing.

*Problems of Urban and Minority Youth.* No summary of issues facing the nation in the new millennium can neglect the acute problems facing urban and minority youth. The salience of the demographic changes and concomitant growth in minority population were discussed previously. However, special attention must be focused on the shocking reality that almost one-half of African-American teenagers have no jobs and that youth unemployment generally remains inordinately high — more than twice the overall unemployment figure for the country. And dropout rates are close to 50% in many of our urban school districts. These two factors point up the danger of our urban schools becoming, in one college president's words, "warehouses for the angry or staging areas for anarchy."

In addition to the morally compelling arguments for equality and equity of educational opportunities, reasons of self-interest must compel us to address the problems of urban and minority youth. As mentioned earlier, our population is aging, and shrinking cohorts of young people must be productive to generate the revenues necessary to support services in a changing economy. More of these youngsters obviously will be of minority origin. They represent valuable human resources that our nation can ill-afford to waste.

*Achieving Quality and Accountability.* There has been growing concern for greater accountability and quality in every facet of American life, from manufactured goods and services to schools. Recent education reform initiatives have decried, for example, "the rising tide of mediocrity" or the "lack of standards" in our schools. While acknowledging the very positive thrust of the standards movement (which, it is hoped, will persist into the 21st century), we cannot afford to retreat from our national commitment to the interrelated issues of equity and equality of educational opportunity. Unfortunately, that commitment seems to be ebbing. Quality does not preclude equity, or vice versa. These two transcendent goals are complementary and support each other. The consequences to our society of emphasizing one at the expense of the other will be particularly grave because of the economic and demographic imperatives already discussed. At the same time, we must acknowledge that the quality of many of our institutions has become shoddy, and so a parallel commitment to quality is essential.

*Foreign Language Instruction.* Another often ignored issue is the appalling decline in language training in the United States. In a shrinking world with an interdependent global economy, a persuasive case can be made that our competitive position is weakened by the deterioration both in quality and quantity of our foreign language instruction. Many Japanese and Europeans, for example, know and speak our language, whereas the numbers of our citizens able to converse in other tongues is abysmally small. Our businesses thus have a distinct disadvantage compared to their foreign competitors in such areas as marketing and sales, in spite of the growing prevalence of English as the international language of trade and diplomacy.

The statistics tell the story more graphically than words. Only 10% to 15% of our high school students currently study foreign languages beyond the second year, and just 8% of our institutions of higher education require students to have studied a foreign language. In 1966, 34% of the institutions required such instruction for admission. These shocking numbers should encourage us to welcome many new citizens who have the advantage of speaking languages other than English. These new residents can prove to be a valuable economic resource as we seek to improve our international economic position.

*Relationships Between Elementary-Secondary and Higher Education.* Another issue that will require increased attention by education policy makers in the future will be the need to more closely coordinate elementary-secondary and higher education. The twelfth grade has been a mystical dividing line between the two, and efforts must be expanded to more effectively bridge the levels in areas where they overlap. We no longer can afford duplicative programs. For example, many community colleges offer remedial and vocational programs, under the aegis of adult basic education, that are nearly identical to the offerings

19

of school systems. Mechanisms must be created at the local or regional level that will more explicitly coordinate elementary-secondary and higher education.

Also, we ought to move away from categorical set-asides and blatant political trade-offs that temporarily "buy" peace between the levels. If educators do not take the initiative in coordinating their systems, politicians certainly will in a time of declining resources. As the competition for dollars becomes keener, there is a real danger of dysfunctional inter-level conflict both for government and private funds. For example, in the area of private and corporate giving, where higher education historically has had the terrain to itself, there are trends that could generate negative competition between the levels. The public schools recently have turned to the private sector for support, and local and regional foundations are being created throughout the country to serve as the conduits for contributions.

Although there has been little or no overt interlevel conflict thus far, the dangers of this occurring are all too real. Politicians are the first to say that conflict within a policy realm such as education could hurt everyone, particularly at a time when resources will be harder to find and competition is keener. Education leaders from all segments of the enterprise have a responsibility to ensure that such interlevel conflicts do not arise.

*The Federal Role in Shaping Education Policy.* The appropriate role of the federal government in shaping education policy will remain a persistent and controversial issue, as the actions of the 104th Congress dramatically reflect. International political and economic issues appear to require national responses. It seems unlikely that 50 states, some 15,000 local school systems, and more than 3,200 postsecondary education institutions have the human or economic resources for the expensive research and development investments that must be made in the new technologies, science, math, foreign language, and computer education. The necessary technological crash programs and heavy up-front investments needed in such new areas as computer education must be promulgated at the federal level as we compete in an international economy against countries such as Japan and West Germany, which have national planning.

Although there are doubtless excesses in some of the education initiatives undertaken by the federal government in recent years, the realities of the 21st century will require our nation to find some middle ground between federal domination and programmatic and substantive voids in technical areas that the country cannot afford. Indeed, our concerns with such areas as math, science, and technology should serve as lightning rods, as all segments of the society acknowledge a common stake in setting national priorities and creating a balanced federalism in order to compete economically and to maximize the development of our human capital.

## Conclusion

I have attempted to provide an environmental scan of a number of salient social, political, and economic issues that I believe will influence education policy in the 21st century. Indeed, my overarching thesis is that the future success of our schools will in no small measure be determined by larger social and economic forces that inexorably drive public and education policy. Recent reform initiatives offer unique opportunities because of the interest in improving education manifested by governors, business and civic leaders, and other influential political figures. However, economic support will be forthcoming only if taxpayers are convinced — rather quickly — that there are tangible results of their increased investment as measured by improved student performance.

In fact, the reform movement already may have crested; and there will be an urgent need in the immediate future to sort out the various reforms and determine which have been most effective on a cost-benefit basis. The future of public education in the 21st century may well be determined by the results.

# THE CHAMELEON'S DISH, PROMISE-CRAMMED

## by Stanley Elam

*Stanley M. Elam is editor emeritus of the* Phi Delta Kappan. *For more than a quarter-century, he has coordinated the Phi Delta Kappa/Gallup polls, recently summarizing that experience in a new book,* How America Views Its Schools *(PDK, 1995). "The Chameleon's Dish" was a serial personal column that Stan wrote for the* Kappan *during 1970-71, while on sabbatical in Washington, D.C., as interim editor of the* NASSP Bulletin.

Thwack! It's the distinctive sound of persimmon on Balata, heard perhaps two million times a day, I would guess, on the 1,098 golf courses of Florida, where I now live.

Until recently, that is. Today you're far more likely to hear the ping of metal on Surlyn. Even in the tradition-bound game of golf, change is a constant. And as people continue to pursue pleasure and the bitch goddess success into the next century, the pace of change will no doubt accelerate. Being 79 years old, I may not see the next century, of course. Among the few things one can still count on are mortality, taxes, and junk mail — but they're working on all of these.

In this brief and very personal essay, I want to examine some of the more significant changes I have witnessed over 75 years as a participant-observer on the education scene. And perhaps I'll venture a few predictions.

For me, it all started in 1920, when my father got the teacher's permission (no problem — Dad was a school director) to send me trotting down the hill behind my older brother to Wabash School. The little school building, a coal shed, and two outhouses sat on a corner of our 80-acre subsistence farm in south-central Illinois. At age 4, I was a sort of latch-key kid, although in those days nobody in Big Spring Township ever locked his front door. My mother was dead at age 36, and Dad was

23

trying to farm while cooking, cleaning, canning, sewing, tending five kinds of farm animals, making a garden, and caring for two small boys.

Guy V. Storm taught 40 youngsters, aged 6 to 15, in all eight grades during an eight-hour day. He was interrupted only by two 15-minute recesses and a lunch hour. For his work, he was paid about $60 a month, like nearly 8,000 other one-room rural teachers in Illinois. Later on, Guy was fired — my father's influence again — for expecting too little academically, for maintaining only lax discipline, and for inflating our grades. In short, he was way ahead of his time. Guy left teaching and became a wealthy insurance broker. Thanks, Dad.

Let me describe this one-room rural school. There were, of course, pictures of Washington and Harding on the wall above the blackboard, close beside a reproduction of *The Angelus* and a Regulator clock. The floors were splintered pine, oiled to lay the dust. There was a cast iron stove in one corner and shelves for perhaps 75 books in another. This "library" was purchased with profits from school-sponsored pie suppers and egg roasts. There were phonics charts and a set of Rand McNally maps on the rostrum across the front of the room, flanking the teacher's desk.

The younger children sat at small desks on the left, and the desks got progressively larger up to grade eight on the right. Every five minutes or so a class would shuffle to the front bench for recitations. On Friday afternoons we had spell-downs, geography contests, and arithmetic competition at the blackboard. Maybe once a year, the county superintendent would visit and do a little politicking. (He was an elected official.) At Christmas time, the teacher treated us all with sacks of candy and large California navel oranges — the only oranges some of us would eat all winter. At recess and noon hour, we played blackman, dare base, one-hole cat (using a homemade yarn baseball), and, after Henry Riney succeeded Guy Storm, basketball on the dirt court.

I loved the place. So much so that I resented having to go home for lunch while the other kids ate their meals from brown bags or battered pails. I sneaked into the building during summer vacations to read Zane Grey (*The Young Forester* was my favorite), Horatio Alger's Ragged Dick stories, and a series of Tom Slade adventures. When I finished the school library, I was ready for Dad's complete works of Charles Dickens and even sampled his Dante's *Inferno*, but my only memory of it is Gustave Dore's marvelous etchings of nearly naked men and women burning or freezing in Hell.

Of the 80 or more farm children I knew in grade school, no more than half a dozen went on to high school, and I was the only one from my Wabash class to finish. In those days — the Depression Thirties — high school wasn't considered very important in a farming community and, in any case, getting there wasn't easy. Mostly, I rode horseback the six miles to Stewardson District High School, about 25 minutes aboard Old Red. In the four-teacher, one-coach school of 115 students, the curriculum consisted of four years of English, three of math (algebra, geometry, and a semester each of advanced algebra and trigonometry), three years of science (general, biology, and physics), American history, civics, two years of Latin, typing and shorthand, bookkeeping, two years of "manual training," and, as I remember, four years of physical education twice a week. The teacher tossed out a ball and left the gym. No art or music was offered, although I remember occasional "music appreciation" radio programs. No agriculture or home economics. No chemistry. No modern foreign language. Supervised extracurricular activities were limited to basketball, baseball, and track (football proved too expensive), all for boys only. Class plays were produced in the junior and senior years. That was it.

But again, I loved it. Perhaps too much. I neglected my chores at home in order to take part in sports and the plays. I studied and read and wrote. It was too much for Dad. He "invited" me to leave, and I accepted. For two days I stayed with cousin and classmate Dale Haverstock. There were no school counselors, of course, but I.K. Jurgensmeyer, the high school principal, mediated the argument. When I promised to gather the eggs and feed the chickens regularly, I was allowed to return home.

Four years later, I was a principal and teacher in an even smaller, three-year high school only an hour's drive from my home town. I was one of perhaps half the graduates of Eastern Illinois State Teachers College (now Eastern Illinois University) to get a teaching job that year. My qualifications were a wife (principals were married men, teachers single women), a willingness to compromise my better judgment, and meeting Illinois minimums for teaching high school history and social studies, English, science, math, and Latin. I taught them all, staying one page ahead of the kids. Seven classes, seven preparations, one free period. I also used my car as a school bus, coached basketball and softball teams, advised student publications, and served as Scoutmaster. Noting my willingness to do *anything* to please, no matter how badly I did it, the grade school teachers and the other high school teacher insisted that I practice singing hymns with them so that we could perform at funerals and weddings. A long-time Jewett faculty tradition, they told me. It was weeks before I caught on.

I left Jewett when my master's degree was in sight and a four-year high school principalship beckoned. And I left that job for a superintendency as soon as I could find one. In each school I also taught a variety of courses and coached boys' sports. The war was consuming young men like a Jules Verne maelstrom. Small schools unwilling to advance women to administration were forced to hire rank amateurs like myself.

I have a twinge even today when I recall the frustrations of those years. In the education courses I took, professors who hadn't seen the inside of a small rural school in decades, if ever, expounded theories I couldn't possibly use. Like my small-school colleagues, I did whatever it took to get by.

Coaching demanded an inordinate amount of time. I had inherited several talented basketball players in a hoop-crazy county with some 20 small high schools. In the regular season we won 23 games and lost three, all by the margin of three points — and all to the same team, which had less talent but better coaching. I lay awake nights replaying those three games, and won them all. Then came the sectional match-up, and who was our opponent? The same three-time nemesis. Two days before the game, Connie Porterfield, my 220-pound center, smashed my foot in a scrimmage (he needed competition and I tried to provide it). The next day Connie severed his Achilles tendon in an auto accident. We lost, 36-33.

The following week some enterprising student printed "Dope" in the dust on the rear window of my car. In those days the word meant something about half-way between klutz and nerd, not quite a fool but cognitively challenged. Impractical. In short, dopey.

Wiping off the back window of my car, I plunged into agonizing reappraisal. I recalled a confession once made to me by my all-time favorite college professor, Kevin Guinagh. A classicist whose translations of Latin literature were standard, Guinagh also wrote popular works (*Inspired Amateurs* and *Search for Glory*). His droll wit made the study of college Latin a delight. But Guinagh once took a leave of absence from Eastern Illinois to teach at Antioch College, the experimental school, at a time when Antioch was testing student evaluations of faculty. He told me he returned to Charleston largely because one of his students wrote, "Looks and acts like a clown."

I was seeking perspective. I asked myself, Can you, should you, go on faking it? Will you ever find a job in education that you can do well and still earn enough to support a wife and family? The answers weren't clear. So, telling myself that I was missing the great world event of my life, I drove to St. Louis and took the exams for a Navy commission. I learned I had *pes planus* (or flat feet, one having been made more *planus* by Connie Porterfield), but I passed the physical anyway. Then a Lt. Carey told me I also had made the highest score ever recorded at the St. Louis recruiting office on the SAT-type Navy officer screening exam. That's what teaching history, civics, math, science, Latin, and English will do for you. My self-esteem somewhat restored, I reported for duty three days after commencement in 1944, thus escaping from education — or so I thought.

Actually, I spent the next two years as a student and teacher, but in less pressure-laden circumstances.

Of the 12 radiomen and signalmen I trained for Navy communications, 10 used the GI Bill to attend college. (I lost track of the other two.) I rank the GI Bill with the Northwest Ordinance of 1787, the Morrill Act of 1862, and the Smith-Hughes Act of 1917 as the most beneficent forms of federal intervention ever in what the Founding Fathers thought was a function reserved to the states. (I used the bill myself to get a doctor's degree without going bankrupt.) By the time I became editor of the *Phi Delta Kappan* in 1956, postsecondary education at least partially at government expense was almost as commonplace as a free high school education was for my generation. The U.S. continued to extend its system of colleges and universities until today it is the envy of the world.

Yet we are now at a crossroads in the history of higher education. Will we continue to maintain access to ever-broader constituencies, or will a college education be restricted to those whose parents can afford it or who are lucky and smart enough to win scholarships? I hope the popular will is consulted on this pregnant question. In 1974, the PDK/Gallup education poll tells us, 85% of the public believed that a college education was at that time either "extremely important" or "fairly important" for young people's success in life. A decade later this number had risen to 89%. Almost no one in either poll said a college education is unimportant.

In 1982, the poll showed that 87% of the parents of public school children would like to have their children go on to college, giving as reasons more job opportunities, better income, and the need for more education today to cope with life's problems. Yet, even in 1982, only 57% of these same public school parents thought their children *would* attend college. In 1989, the poll showed that 83% of the public favored more state and federal assistance for otherwise able and willing students who could not afford college. Finally, in 1993, 81% of all poll respondents favored President Clinton's proposal for a national service program (now in place in a limited form) that would help young people pay for college by working in a public service position for a year or two. All demographic groups, including both Democrats and Republicans, favored the proposal.

One of the most serious challenges to social and political leadership in the next century will be to provide access to higher education for all young people who can use it — the poor as well as the rich, women as well as men, minorities as well as the majority. It is both a social and economic imperative for the post-industrial age.

Knowledge is good. Knowledge is power. Knowledge is money. Knowledge is the chocolate layer-cake you can eat and have too. If we don't give everyone equal access to it, we are likely to have an ever-widening disparity between the haves and have-nots, more elitism and conspicuous consumption, more racial conflict as minorities become the majority before the year 2100, more social chaos, and another million incarcerated young people — the continuing scandal of modern-day America. Ultimately — in the absence of political leaders as imaginative as FDR and his Brain Trust, who dreamed up the CCC, the NYA, Social Security, and dozens of other ameliorative programs during the Great Depression — we could have class warfare and something akin to the Nazism of pre-war Germany. Or so I believe.

\* \* \*

By 1950, every one of the six public schools I attended or taught in while growing up had disappeared, victims of the consolidation movement that reduced the number of school districts in America from well over 100,000 to the 15,000 of today. The public and most of the education profession praised people like James B. Conant, the Harvard ex-president and all-purpose guru who recommended elimination of small high schools. Sidney Marland, the charismatic school administrator and Nixon appointee as U.S. Commissioner of Education in 1970, even developed the idea of vast education parks, a concept he proposed for Pittsburgh in his Great High Schools Program. It called for the construction of five "super" high schools, each with approximately 6,000 students. The Pitt board had the good sense to reject it.

I have a letter from the late Gordon I. Swanson, a past president of Phi Delta Kappa, in which he calls Conant the most destructive education leader of our century. Swanson knew that small schools were the cement that held many rural communities together. In vast, impersonal urban high schools the average anonymous student tends to get lost. He may find security and a home in a neighborhood gang. Personal relationships between students and teachers and individual attention are unusual. It now seems obvious that consolidation bred many unintended consequences. The next century is likely to usher in many changes to restore a sense of community and closer, longer-term student-teacher ties in the education process and to shift more responsibility from bureaucratic central administration to the school site.

By lucky chance, as an undergraduate I came under the influence of a clever and charming English professor who advised student publications. I remember two pieces of advice Franklyn Andrews offered repeatedly: "Keep evergreen on top" and "The mark of a civilized person is suspended judgment." These are words to live by for an education journal editor who tries to deal with controversy. I had them in mind when I asked the Phi Delta Kappa board, in 1960, to support a *Kappan* policy of treating education issues vigorously, offering readers all sides as fairly and objectively as we could. The board agreed, and they backed me solidly when a National Education Association executive secretary, offended by an article questioning NEA qualifications as a leader in the teacher collective negotiations movement, tried to get me fired. The treatment of controversial issues is still the anchor of *Kappan* editorial policy.

At some point in the early Sixties, I framed six question categories into which all perennial education controversies can be fitted:

Who will teach?
Who will be taught?
What will be taught?
How will we teach?
How will teaching be organized, controlled, and financed?

Obviously, there's no space here to deal with all of these issues, even sketchily. But let's look at just the first question for a moment. Every year, more than one million bachelor's degrees are awarded by U.S. colleges and universities. Since 1986, about 10% of them have been in education. Most of the education graduates who enter teaching will get a master's degree if they remain in education, and a relatively small number will go on for the doctorate.

We still have only crude measures of the promise of competence in teaching or, for that matter, of competence in any profession. But those we do have tell us that, on average, teaching majors are among the weakest in the college crop. Their SATs are lower and so are their grades in academic courses. The brightest, most energetic, and most ambitious young people are more likely to be attracted to medicine,

29

law, engineering, and science, which usually are thought of as more intellectually demanding fields.

These disparities are not hard to understand. It's true that the public values the contributions educators make to society (more than any profession other than medicine and the ministry). It's true that a majority of people responding to PDK/Gallup polls say they would be glad to have their children become teachers (wealthier respondents are an exception). But it's also true that the system of rewards and the working conditions we offer teachers are among the worst in the industrialized world. (The vast majority of poll respondents concede that U.S. teachers are poorly paid.)

Adjusted for inflation, teacher salaries, on average, have advanced little since Guy Storm made $60 a month teaching at Wabash School. *The Condition of Education*, 1993 edition, shows that median starting salaries for education graduates were lower than those for graduates in any other field of study in 1986 — a full 18.6% below the median for all college grads. By 1990, they had risen a bit but still placed education graduates on the bottom rung.

Occupational status is closely related to occupational income, so there is a vicious cycle here. It is my belief that a benevolent cycle could be established if teacher salaries were made competitive with those in, say, engineering. If the nearly three million public school teachers of America, whose salaries now total about 100 billion dollars, were suddenly given $125 billion, the rush of bright, energetic, ambitious college students to the schools and departments of education would be on. And if opportunities for advancement that do not remove teachers from the classroom were made available, the present 10.5-year average career of teachers would double in one generation.

Will it happen? I doubt it.

But something of the sort *could* happen in the next century. It would be a promising start if the National Education Association and the American Federation of Teachers should combine forces and gain greater control over access to the education profession, much as the American Medical Association and the American Bar Association influence access to medicine and law. Twenty years of collective negotiations in education have been generally disappointing as a lever to advance teacher salaries and welfare. But by merging, as the AFL and CIO did two generations ago, the NEA and AFT could reverse the trend. Achieving such a merger will be enormously difficult, given NEA/AFT organizational dynamics. Yet I remain convinced that a huge infusion of the best and brightest young people into the public schools, a phenomenon that such a merger could promote, might do more to improve public education, ultimately, than all of the panaceas now being advanced in the name of reform.

\* \* \*

I started this rambling essay with some imagery from the game of golf, whose basic rules haven't changed much over the past century, although the equipment used and the techniques of instruction have. The governing bodies of golf quite properly fear revolutionary change. In education, dozens of innovations have been introduced during my lifetime. Among them are school consolidation, busing, nursery schools and publicly supported kindergarten, racial desegregation, curriculum updates by the score, individually prescribed instruction for the handicapped, bilingual instruction, junior and community colleges, and so on. Elsewhere I have listed more than 80 such changes that have been almost universally adopted. Most of them have been initiated *within* the profession, not forced from outside. And most of them have been improvements. They have extended access, equalized opportunity, increased efficiency — all without affecting the essential character of our free, publicly supported school system as the engine and bulwark of democracy. Our education system is copied everywhere that people have discovered a basic property of democracy: It is the only self-correcting form of government and social control.

But some of the changes now being trumpeted in the name of reform, to "save our failing school system," would subvert the basic rules that undergird democratic education. Among these so-called reforms are government vouchers to pay for education in private and parochial schools not accountable to democratically elected representatives, privatization that would further the crass commercialization of American life, and other measures that can only increase elitism and class, race, and economic divisions. We have enough of those already.

# CIVIC DISENGAGEMENT AND THE ATTACK ON PUBLIC EDUCATION

by Donovan R. Walling

*Donovan R. Walling is editor of Special Publications at Phi Delta Kappa. A long-time public school teacher and administrator in Wisconsin and Indiana, he is the author of two books, four PDK fastbacks, and numerous articles on education topics, in addition to poetry and drama. Donovan was appointed to the PDK Headquarters staff in 1993 to head Special Publications, an activity of the Phi Delta Kappa Educational Foundation.*

Much of the 20th century has seen a conscious, pervasive effort at all levels to enlarge the social connectedness of American society. Since 1900, the currents of public awareness (albeit not without exception) have rippled in ever-widening, more inclusive circles, empowering the powerless to participate in the mainstream of social and political life and enfranchising the disenfranchised.

Women's suffrage, black civil rights, women's liberation, gay civil rights, and other social struggles have transformed not merely the face of American life but also its deepest structures. However, a counter-current of parochialism and elitism has been ever-present. In the final years of this century, that counter-current appears to be ascending in prominence and influence in direct relation to a quarter-century decline in American social connectedness.

Roger Putnam, writing in the *Journal of Democracy* (1995), reports a steady erosion of Americans' civic engagement. He notes that the number of Americans who report attending a public meeting "on town or school affairs" fell by more than a third in the 20 years from 1973 to 1993. Parent-teacher association (PTA) membership, an indicator of parent involvement in schools, fell dramatically from more than 12 million members in 1964 to a low of 5 million in 1982, rising to about 7 million now. Membership in fraternal organizations (Lions, Elks, Shriners, Masons) is universally in decline. Membership in the Jaycees, for example, is off by 44% since 1979 (pp. 68-70).

Putnam comments that:

> more Americans than ever before are in social circumstances that foster associational involvement (higher education, middle age, and so on), but nevertheless aggregate associational membership appears to be stagnant or declining. (p. 72)

Asking "Why is U.S. social capital eroding?" Putnam posits four possible explanations:

- Movement of women into the labor force, which is "the primary, though not the sole, reason why the weekly working hours of the average American have increased significantly";
- Mobility, which has reduced the "social rootedness" that encourages civic engagement;
- Other demographic transformations, such as "fewer marriages, more divorces, fewer children, and lower real wages," which have undermined civic engagement by eroding personal time and resources; and
- The "technological transformation of leisure," by which electronic technology has "individualized" the use of leisure time at the expense of social interaction (pp. 74-75).

The decline in civic engagement has broad implications. Disengagement from social connectedness undermines institutions such as schools, which are social compacts that depend on civic engagement and civic trust. The decline in civic trust is nowhere more evident than in matters related to the public schools.

Early in the 1980s, a misguided political initiative largely aimed at making public education the scapegoat for society's ills resulted in the publication of *A Nation at Risk: The Imperative for Educational Reform* (1983). The purpose of the National Commission on Excellence in Education was to "define the problems afflicting American education" (p. iii), thus focusing entirely on the negatives rather than the positives of American schooling. As a consequence of this negative purpose, the resulting report presented a narrow, distorted, and in some instances, flatly wrong view of public education.

This document became a clarion call to critics of every ilk. And while the criticism frequently has been unfounded, biased, or politically motivated, some good has come about in schools because of the increased attention paid to them. Certainly no institution, however effective, can meet the continuing needs of its constituency without attending to self-evaluation and improvement. Focusing attention on the schools by means of a public spotlight has encouraged and supported some improvements that might otherwise not have occurred.

However, a number of subsequent studies, including the meta-analyses by researcher Gerald Bracey that have been published in a recent series of annual reports in the *Phi Delta Kappan*, have demonstrated that American public schools have improved fairly consistently over the course of this century. In fact, they never were as bad as they were characterized in *A Nation at Risk*, which gave us the memorable slur that "the educational foundations of our society are presently being eroded by a rising tide of mediocrity" (p. 5).

The most unfortunate consequence of *A Nation at Risk* and its aftermath is the loss of civic trust in public education. That loss is enormous. In this regard the critics — even the well-meaning ones — have done a disservice to the nation. Frequently, the critics of public education have proposed "solutions" that, if implemented, will further weaken public education, such as vouchers to allow students to attend private or religious schools on public money. More often than not, the alternatives to public education that are touted by pundits and politicians are elitist and involve — sometimes subtly, sometimes blatantly — the segregation of students by class, race, or sex.

In undermining confidence in public education as a civic institution, those who have attacked and continue to attack public education strike at the very heart of democracy. It was John Adams, the second President of the United States, who perhaps stated the premise most clearly: "The whole people must take upon themselves the education of the whole people and must be willing to bear the expense of it."

R. Freeman Butts, in *The Education of the West* (1973), recounted the early tide of civic engagement in education in the decade after independence:

> Samuel Knox, Samuel Harrison Smith, Benjamin Rush, and Robert Coram among others stated the case for modernizing American education. Education should be universally free in order to provide equal opportunity for all individuals as well as to prepare citizens for their responsibilities in a democracy. It should embrace a comprehensive system of elementary, secondary, and higher institutions under national control in order to contribute to secular rather than religious outcomes and to ensure the greatest progress toward social welfare. (pp. 405-406)

National control did not come about because of the strong tradition of decentralized control of education. But the intent of the earliest national leaders is clear. Only a freely available, comprehensive, secular system of education can ensure that democracy will flourish and that the American society will prosper. It is to this end that public education has been dedicated.

In the closing years of the 20th century, the most influential countercurrent to this democratic social proposition has come from the so-called Religious Right. Putnam notes that Americans' engagement in organized religion has modestly declined since mid-century, perhaps by a sixth since the 1960s (p. 69). Yet in the wake of this general disengagement from religion, a vigorous fundamentalist minority has coalesced. Swept up by ideological fervor, the Religious Right cloaks its starkly undemocratic ambitions in moralistic rhetoric. Its leaders speak of "family values" as if by proprietary right.

Only the most naive will fail to see that the Religious Right worships most fervently at the altar of political clout and envisions an America in which public education — if indeed education is to remain "public" at all — is reshaped to radical fundamentalist ends. George Kaplan (1994a) characterizes the Religious Right in this way:

> they are not above distorting the truth, often by misrepresenting who they are at election time or by portraying opponents, many of them pillars of their communities, as anti-family extremists.
>
> While soft-pedaling their preference for a theocratic America, the grandees of the Religious Right are campaigning for exactly that. As long as they can get away with mislabeling themselves — most tellingly to the millions of decent religious fundamentalists who care deeply about their children's upbringing — the more likely they are to continue their recent advances. (p. 52)

The Religious Right (or Christian Right) rose to prominence as a political force in the 1980 election of Ronald Reagan to the U.S. presidency. By the mid- to late-1980s, according to Kaplan (1994b), the movement had begun to be "dismissed by political pundits and mainline religious spokespersons as a collection of buffoonish has-beens" (p. K1). But by the mid-1990s, the Religious Right had re-emerged "better organized, more sharply focused, and much wiser in the ways of postmodern secular society" (p. K1).

Thus in this last decade of the century, public education in America is faced with a dark vision. According to Kaplan:

> Buttressed by its rigidly interpreted code of beliefs and disillusioned by what it considers to be the growing futility of public edu-

cation, the new Christian Right is seeking to position itself as an arbiter or standard-setter of life in education's household. In the never-ending national conversation about what and how our children are to learn, it has staked out a clear moral stance: its version of true, uncompromising Christian belief, which it defends with primitive ferocity. (1994*b*, p. K2)

Although Kaplan sees no takeover of public education by the Religious Right, he does envision an ongoing battle:

> In district after district, supporters of the schools are finding themselves on the defensive, often unable to rally lasting support for venturesome but sound educational practices. Unless and until this backing materializes and becomes a permanent feature of the educational landscape, the promoters of reactionary political causes and outdated educational doctrine will continue their advance in the nation's schools. (1994*b*, p. K12)

The future of American public education must be built in the new century — in the new millennium — on this note of caution. Public education must embody the civic currents and social traditions that stretch back to our nation's founding.

## Education Beyond the Year 2000

From the standpoint of student achievement, today's schools are better than they ever were in the past. There is sufficient unbiased evidence to confidently make this statement, in spite of political rhetoric to the contrary. But public education has indeed failed in one key area — that is, in the maintenance of the public dialogue necessary for encouraging and sustaining civic trust and civic engagement.

Jean Jacques Rousseau, the 16th century French philosopher who influenced the ideas of many early American political leaders, wrote eloquently of this essential proposition of democracy. In his 1762 book, *The Social Contract*, he delineated the necessity of collaborative civic engagement in this way:

> *Each of us places in common his person and all his power under the supreme direction of the general will; and as one body we all receive each member as an indivisible part of the whole.*
>
> From that moment, instead of as many separate persons as there are contracting parties, this act of association produces a moral and collective body, composed of as many members as there are votes in the assembly, which from this act receives its unity, its common self, its life, and its will. . . .

Man loses by the social contract his *natural* liberty, and an unlimited right to all which tempts him, and which he can obtain; in return he acquires *civil* liberty, and proprietorship of all he possesses. . . . In addition, we might add to the other acquisition of the civil state that of moral liberty, which alone renders a man master of himself; for it is *slavery* to be under the impulse of mere appetite, and *freedom* to obey a law which we prescribe for ourselves. (Black, Lottich, and Seckinger 1972, pp. 454-57)

The philosophy that underpins American democracy must be considered together with the educational, social, political, and technological trends of this century. Only from this confluence can an observer draw out a vision of the future of American public education. Therefore, looking forward into the 21st century, the question must be asked in a new form: How should democracy be preserved through public education?

Many politicians and educators are preoccupied with the lesser question of preserving the public schools and making public education a better servant. These concerns are important, but they miss the real point. The problem is not that public education is under attack, but rather that democracy is under attack.

No direct assault on the body of American democracy is necessary when the simple pinching off of an important blood vessel or one key nerve is sufficient to render the body incapable of self-defense. Public education is that blood vessel, that nerve. Control of public education is one means to control the nation. If the public schools reflect and teach the ideals of a democratic society, then the democracy may flourish. If the public schools are fragmented, if the curriculum is rendered in narrow and parochial terms, if freedom and diversity are constrained, then democracy is diminished, and factionalism is substituted for freedom.

It is ironic that the authors of *A Nation at Risk* wrote, "If an unfriendly foreign power had attempted to impose on America the mediocre educational performance that exists today, we might well have viewed it as an act of war." In fact, a decidedly unfriendly, albeit domestic, power — namely the Religious Right — is attempting to impose a narrow, exclusionary, distorted vision on America through the political process at all levels and, in particular, through local elections to school boards in order to fundamentally reshape public education at the grassroots. This insidious attack is nothing less than an act of war on American democracy.

This attack has been allowed to proceed, in part, because schools have not responded adequately to the factors enumerated by Putnam.

Public education did not create the social forces or the technology that Putnam cites as contributing to civic disengagement. Nor would public education have been able to control these elements had education leaders foreseen their consequences. But public education, had it embodied a keener understanding of the civic necessities for producing and maintaining a democracy, might have mitigated the current crisis.

Only now, in the midst of battle, are education leaders coming to grips with the "novel" notion of public involvement in public education. The "we-they" mentality of educators versus others — an elementary-secondary version of "town and gown" — has ill-served students and the education profession in the past. Perpetuation of this mentality now endangers the very existence of public education.

Thus the future of public education will be shaped by how well school people now involve their constituents in responding to educational, social, political, and technological challenges. With this in mind, it may be useful to suggest some responses. Following are possibilities related to the Putnam's four factors in civic disengagement:

*Women in the workforce.* The chief effect felt by educators is the increased likelihood that both parents of any given student will work outside the home. Few single parents, mothers or fathers, have ever been able to stay at home. However, as more women in two-parent families also have entered the workforce, the stay-at-home mom who had time to volunteer in the school, to supervise after-school activities, or simply to be home to greet her returning children has become increasingly rare.

Many schools have yet to take positive steps to accommodate this change that has been a fact of life for nearly half a century. Women's "liberation" (after the initial suffrage period of the 1910s and 1920s) actually surged during World War II. In the aftermath of that war, women who had taken wartime jobs returned to the home in fewer numbers than had previous generations after earlier wars. The momentum of this postwar employment pattern escalated to become the more visible women's liberation movement of the late 1960s. Instead of recognizing this trend and developing alternative ways to keep parents involved, school leaders in many cases chose simply to lament the lack of parent involvement. For far too long, blaming the parents has been an accepted response.

*Mobility.* Modern America is a nation on the move — and has been for most of this century. In fact, since 1948, when the first mobility sta-

39

tistics were recorded, approximately 20% of the U.S. population has moved annually. That amounts to about 40 million people each year (Walling 1990). Yet few schools recognize this mobility unless it involves defined groups, such as immigrants, refugees, or military children. Corporate mobility, which accounts for a significant number of family moves, continues to be largely unnoticed. More important, mobility is seldom taken into account in school plans for curriculum, student orientation, parent involvement, or other matters.

Simply recognizing the shifting population base in most communities would be a step toward seeing and addressing the needs of newcomers and transients. When such recognition is not forthcoming, those who are "invisible" become marginalized and often alienated. Public education makes no friends in this manner.

*Demographic changes.* Putnam cites "fewer marriages, more divorces, fewer children, and lower real wages." All of these factors bear on the public's ability to interact with schools in traditional ways. Because public school leaders have not accommodated these changing demographics, frustrated citizens are seen as easy converts by those whose political religion thrives on condemning the public schools for their supposed failure to sustain "traditional family values." In fact, those so-called traditional family values have changed because families themselves have changed. Education's failure has been in not recognizing those changes and working to include different kinds of families in the community of public education.

The profound failure in all areas — society, politics, education — to reconceptualize the American family substitutes breast beating for solution seeking. Public approbation of the doomsayers encourages only more and louder breast beating and less real work toward resolving the problems. A requirement for this real work will be a new foundation based on reality, rather than on the myth of the traditional family. The reality is that families must be regarded as collectivities that are based on a number of relational variables: biological, affectional, legal, and economic.

*Technology and the transformation of leisure.* Perhaps the most pervasive transformation — and the one least amenable to accommodation by school people — is the "individualization" of leisure that disconnects humans from social interaction. However, schools that view technology not merely as a way to do old work faster but as a way to do new work, to reconceptualize activities, can explore — and in many cases already

40

are using — technological strategies for reconnecting people.

At the simplest level, homework hotlines provide a quasi-human connection between parent or student and teacher. Parents who once had time to stop by the classroom for homework information but whose schedules no longer permit such contacts at least can "connect" with the teacher's voice. The electronic link between school and home may be weak, but it is better than no link at all. Only slightly more sophisticated technology using audio or video connections permits electronic interactions, such as parent-educator committees that "meet" via telephone conference calls. Again, although they are a poor substitute for face-to-face conferences, such interactions are better than no communication.

Reknitting the social fabric of America is the civic imperative of the 21st century. Politicians and educators who would be leaders in the first years of the new millennium will not preserve American democracy by discarding or diminishing that institution which can, by the application of will, ensure its preservation.

On every penny the Latin motto of the United States serves as a constant reminder of the fundamental requirement of American democracy. "E pluribus unum" — from the many, one — speaks to the essence of our national existence. From the diversity of all Americans, the nation draws its unity, its identity, and its strength. No single faction, no vocal minority can be allowed to fragment the whole. Domination of the many for the advantage of the few is antithetical. It contradicts more than two centuries of progress toward realization of the American democratic ideals of inclusivity, equity, and equality.

The answer to the question of how democracy should be preserved through public education is that educators must work to make the schools places that uphold these democratic ideals, that impart them and their importance to students, and, most important, that engender and enlarge civic engagement. By reconnecting the public to their schools, the American system of freely available, comprehensive, secular education can help ensure that democracy will flourish and that the American society will prosper in the 21st century.

## References

Black, Hugh C.; Lottich, Kenneth V.; and Seckinger, Donald S. *The Great Educators.* Chicago: Nelson-Hall, 1972.

Butts, R. Freeman. *The Education of the West.* New York: McGraw-Hill, 1973.

Kaplan, George R. "Deceptions and Fallacies of the Religious Right," *Education Week*, 2 November 1994, pp. 60, 52. a

Kaplan, George R. "Shotgun Wedding." *Phi Delta Kappan* 75 (May 1994): K1-K12. b

National Commission on Excellence in Education. *A Nation At Risk: The Imperative for Educational Reform.* Washington, D.C.: U.S. Government Printing Office, 1993.

Putnam, Robert D. "Bowling Alone: America's Declining Social Capital." *Journal of Democracy* 6 (January 1995): 65-78.

Walling, Donovan R. *Meeting the Needs of Transient Students.* Fastback 304. Bloomington, Ind.: Phi Delta Kappa Educational Foundation, 1990.

# PROFESSIONALS AND POLITICS

## by Jack Frymier

*Jack Frymier currently is the Phi Delta Kappa Senior Fellow. He was a professor of education at Ohio State University for many years, where he also was co-director of the Center for the Study of Motivation and Human Abilities. Jack also served as the national president of the Association for Supervision and Curriculum Development. The author of 11 books and more than 200 articles, Jack's recent research includes the PDK study of students at risk and, currently, a new study of values education.*

Schooling is a human enterprise dedicated to realizing and serving human needs. Like most human ventures, it is characterized by both complexities and inconsistencies. That seems to be the nature of such things.

Positioned in a crucible of social and political concerns, educators who claim — or at least aspire — to be truly professional often find themselves buffeted by politicians and divided by political issues. How should they act? What should they do?

I want to argue that, as individuals, educators should do anything and everything they can — within good conscience — to persuade their fellow humans to adopt those policies, pass those laws, and elect those persons they feel ought to be adopted or passed or elected. However, as members of professional organizations, those same educators should do anything and everything they can to persuade their fellow professionals not to work collectively for the adoption of particular policies or the passage of particular laws or the election of particular people. In other words, I want to argue that professionals, as members of professional organizations, ought not to engage in political activity or political action. Such action diminishes their professional effectiveness and impedes the attainment of professional goals.

"But that is inconsistent," you might say. "It's un-American. It's un-democratic. It violates the spirit of this great nation in every way."

I do not think so. Issues in education, by definition, are unresolved. We do not know the "right" answer to any issue. That ambiguity about what to do is what makes it an issue. When a professional organization adopts a particular position on a political issue — as an organization — such action results in many things, almost none of which are professionally or personally desirable.

If a professional association adopts a stance on a political issue, such action almost always stops further discussion of the issue. It fosters estrangement among members of the association. It alienates the losers, and it diverts the attention of all members from their primary professional purpose to a secondary objective, however important that objective may be. Further, it restricts personal choice among individual members of the association by inducing an unnecessary and inappropriate sense of guilt.

Consider an illustration. Embedded deep within the structure and function of American education is a small group of professional persons banded together into an organization known as Professors of Curriculum. Members of the group like to think of themselves as something of a select group, since membership is restricted to one hundred persons. Over the years, members have come together once or twice a year for a two-day meeting. For purposes of economy and convenience, meetings have traditionally been held prior to the annual meetings of the Association for Supervision and Curriculum Development and the American Educational Research Association, larger organizations whose members' interests and concerns generally parallel those of members of Professors of Curriculum.

In March 1979, the Association for Supervision and Curriculum Development held its annual meeting in Detroit. As usual, Professors of Curriculum was there two days before ASCD officially convened. During the professors' sessions, however, discussion developed about plans for the next year's meeting. The 1980 ASCD meeting was scheduled for Atlanta. Normally, of course, the professors' group would plan to meet two days before the ASCD sessions began, but certain members of Professors of Curriculum complained.

"Georgia has not approved the Equal Rights Amendment," they argued. "We should not go to Georgia for our meeting next year."

Others within the group disagreed: "Our concern is with curriculum. Whether we approve or disapprove of what Georgia does, we ought to hold our meeting in Atlanta, before the ASCD meeting, as always."

In this way, the issue was joined. During the course of the Detroit meeting, tempers flared. Arguments and counter-arguments emerged. Motions were presented. Compromise proposals were developed. Votes were taken. Decisions were made.

Those who urged the organization to "take a stand on the issue and not meet in Atlanta" the following year said, "We have to put pressure on the business community and government leaders in Georgia."

Others replied, "That is not the issue. Who are we to try to pressure legislators from another state? Most of us don't live in Georgia. We have no right to influence their vote. They are not responsible to us. We couldn't vote for them, even if we wanted to."

"But the people in Georgia need to know that if they refuse to support the Equal Rights Amendment, we will go elsewhere for our meetings. We cannot, in good conscience, reward the citizens, politicians, and business leaders of Georgia by meeting in Atlanta and spending our money in the hotels and restaurants there. It's a matter of principle."

"The Constitution of the United States provides a process whereby proposed amendments must be voted up or down by the legislatures of the various states," their opponents argued. "The Georgia legislature, elected by and responsible to the people of Georgia, after extensive debate, voted not to approve the Equal Rights Amendment. Who are we to tell that legislature how they should have voted."

"ERA is an important idea," the others countered. "It should be approved. It should become a part of our Constitution. Those of us who are concerned about curriculum as a means of improving the quality of experience for the young should set an example for others to follow. We should not go to Atlanta next year."

"But we are professors of curriculum. Most of us don't even live in Georgia. To insist that Georgians must agree with us or we will not grace their state presumes that we are right and they are wrong — that we know more than they do — and such a proposition seems arrogant at least and undemocratic at most. As individuals, we should do what our conscience dictates. As a professional organization, we should ignore the problem and meet in Atlanta next year."

In this way the argument unfolded. When the issue was resolved by a vote (the decision was made not to go to Atlanta, but to meet in Washington, D.C., instead), debate stopped, alienation developed among the "losers," and the coercive aspects of the organization's sanctions were seen by some as a violation of members' freedom of choice.

More important, the real purpose of the organization — that which brought the members together in the first place — was relegated to the back burner, while political issues occupied their time. The organization was never a strong organization, professionally, but the debate over political issues rather than curriculum issues frustrated many members and did not lead to a strengthening of the organization except in a narrowing, ideological, non-educational way.

Consider another illustration. In the late 1960s, the Classroom Teachers Association, a division of the National Education Association, initiated efforts to wrest control of the larger organization from the other member groups that were a part of the NEA at that time. The issue was whether NEA should become a political force. By the early 1970s, the Classroom Teachers exercised their numerical muscle, and sub-units such as National Council of Teachers of Mathematics, Music Educators National Conference, Council for Exceptional Children, American Association of School Librarians, Association for Supervision and Curriculum Development, and the American Association of School Administrators, among others, were forced out of the structure and function of NEA and had to set up shop on their own.

In 1976, the National Education Association supported Jimmy Carter's run for the presidency against Gerald Ford, and Carter won. Then in 1980, the NEA supported Carter again in his bid for re-election against Ronald Reagan, but Reagan won. Reagan had vowed during the campaign to abolish the new federal Department of Education, which Carter and the NEA had supported. The NEA tried to exert political pressure against Reagan not the abolish the department. Reagan countered by throwing the full weight of his presidency behind an effort to institute voucher plans in schools and to provide public money for private schools. And in the 15 years since that time, the idea of public support for private schools has become a major Republican agenda item.

The trail of declining public confidence in public education has paralleled the path of the National Education Association's involvement in political activities: The more intensely NEA devoted attention and pressure to political issues, the more negatively the general public has come to view public education, and the more positively the general public has come to view the possibility of using public funds for private schools.

Few Americans and few Republicans want to violate the historic separation of church and state that has existed for more than 200 years. Few Americans and few Republicans think that providing public money to church schools will result in either better schools or better churches. Few Americans want their tax dollars to support private religious groups. But people are angry, and their anger focuses on a teachers union that seems to put its own welfare above the welfare of America's youth.

If the idea and the ideals of public education "go down the drain" in an era of reactionary political backlash, the political activities of so-called professional organizations, such as the National Education Association, will be at least partially responsible for the schools' demise. That would be a tragedy for America — an absolute tragedy. But angry people do unpredictable things, and some Republicans are angry right now. They do not want to destroy America's public school system, but they are angry because certain educators seem more interested in serving their own welfare than they are in serving the public good. Because the National Education Association is such a large organization, all educators may be tainted because that one organization chooses to assume a political rather than a professional posture.

Are there implications in this story for Phi Delta Kappa? What has been Phi Delta Kappa's position on this issue over the years? Let's start by looking back. About 50 years ago, PDK's Handbook on Chapter Activities examined the issue this way:

> One of the most perplexing problems which faces every campus and field chapter is that relating to the kind of policy the chapter shall follow in relation to vital or controversial issues concerning education which develop outside the group, yet affect it. Today perhaps more than ever before, education is confronted with problems so dynamic and so challenging that no individual can ignore them; neither can they be sidetracked by an active group of educators who have any sincere interest whatsoever in the future of their profession. These general questions are further complicated by local issues such as school legislation, tax levies, teacher tenure, and countless others of importance. What shall Phi Delta Kappa's attitude, as reflected in its various chapters, be toward problems of this nature?
>
> There are several possible solutions, any one of which, or in some cases a combination of which, might be adopted by an individual chapter:
>
> 1. Entirely avoid all controversial issues; keep them from appearing on chapter programs and take no stand on either side;
> 2. Allow and encourage discussion on such issues within the chapter . . . but make no effort to influence the attitude of members;
> 3. Discuss controversial issues at meetings. . . and urge each member as an individual to do all he can to bring about the desired end;
> 4. Decide upon which side to support and put the entire chapter, as a group, behind the project;
> 5. Take the initiative, as a group, and make Phi Delta Kappa the sponsor of educational legislation and other educational proposals

in each state; actively back Phi Delta Kappa's participation in state and city politics whenever education is involved.

The first "attitude" suggested above merits little discussion for the reason that it is palpably impossible to carry out in any chapter whose meetings are anything more than social gatherings. . . .

The last proposal, that of encouraging each chapter to act as a unit in taking the initiative in its own state on controversial matters, is not impossible but it seems to be the opinion of chapters themselves (as revealed in the questionnaire sent out by the Committee on Chapter Activities) that it should be discouraged.

The question is still before us. In 1987, at the Biennial Council meeting in Louisville, delegates were asked to support the following policy statement, which had been taken directly from *Phi Delta Kappa: 2000 and Beyond,* a report by the Futures Committee:

> As a private organization, Phi Delta Kappa is beholden to its members, but not beholden to any segment of government, any special interest group, or even any segment of the profession. The independence that accrues to the organization because it has no entangling alliances enables Phi Delta Kappa to establish its own priorities and pursue its only purpose: "to promote quality education."
>
> Phi Delta Kappa should resist all pressures to take positions on political issues. Objectivity is possible only if the independent, non-governmental nature of Phi Delta Kappa is honored by dealing with every issue as an issue — pro and con. Credibility flows to an organization if there is accuracy and lack of bias in its publications and pronouncements. Phi Delta Kappa can assure accuracy and gain credibility only if it refuses to adopt any political stance or support any political position.
>
> Individual members of Phi Delta Kappa should take whatever position they feel is appropriate on any political issue. The organization — as an organization — should continue to provide a forum for dissenting views in education without adopting a political posture or pressuring others into supporting any particular view.

Following a vigorous discussion, the statement was approved. Phi Delta Kappa is on record as committing itself to professional rather than political goals. I think it ought to stay to that professional path.

But what does it mean to be professional? The word implies two things: 1) People who are called "professional" have received special training and possess special skills; and 2) they get paid for helping others with their training and skills. For example, physicians are referred to as professionals because they have had special training and possess special skills, but some athletes are also described as professionals because they get paid for doing what other people do for fun. It's still not clear.

Sociologists have studied professionals as a subgroup of the workforce, and research on the subject of professionalism suggests that those persons and those groups that are truly professional are characterized in six ways.

First, professionals provide service to others; they help other people. But the service provided is not a luxury; it is essential. If a person has a ruptured appendix, for example, that person needs assistance and can not resolve that problem alone.

Second, professionals have special skills and methods that they employ in helping other people, and those skills and methods can be taught and they can be learned. Nobody is born knowing how to counsel an alcoholic, perform a root canal, draw up a contract, or tie a suture. Professional schools teach people how to do those kinds of things.

Third, professionals base what they do on the best research information available. Physicians, for example, do not belong to the Christian Science Church because that church advocates methods of healing that are not empirically verifiable. Every professional group has a solid research base that guides practice.

Fourth, professionals make decisions that affect other people, and the people who are affected usually do not know if the decisions are right or wrong. For example, if a physician tells a patient that he needs open-heart surgery, the patient does not know whether the physician is correct or incorrect. The patient can always get a second opinion, but never really knows whether the proposed procedure is appropriate or required. That means that the possibility for exploitation is always present; clients have to trust what professionals say and do.

Fifth, because the professional-client relationship is based on trust, and because the opportunity for exploitation is always there, every truly professional group has an ethical code. Those persons and groups that are truly professional function under a set of stated ethical principles designed to guarantee that professionals provide the highest quality service to those they help. In that sense, "professional," "ethical," and "effective" are really synonymous terms.

Sixth, those who are truly professional use their professional organization to guarantee that every member of the group adheres to ethical principles. Practitioners who behave in ways that are not in the best interest of clients, or who violate ethical principles, or who conduct a practice based on dogma or personal whim rather than research, are denied the right to practice. Lawyers are disbarred. Physicians lose their right to admit patients to hospitals or their license to practice.

If we convert these characteristics to criteria and apply them to education, we recognize quickly that education has not yet realized its efforts to achieve full professional status. Much remains to be done. That should not discourage us, however. It took physicians thousands of years to achieve truly professional status, and they did not actually achieve that goal until early in this century. We can do it, too, if we set our mind to the task.

The question is: Will pursuing political objectives move us closer or further away from the goal of attaining truly professional status? Do we aspire to political clout or professional expertise? Are we interested in furthering our own interests, or the achievements of young people in the schools? It is easy to say that we ought to be able to do both, but few groups have ever been able to pull that off.

As we move toward the next century, political climates will change, political issues will change, and education issues will change. Let's continue to deal with those issues — as professionals — that are directly related to our areas of professional concern: teaching, learning, curriculum, and the like.

As individuals, we should do whatever we feel is necessary to affect the political issues. Make phone calls. Send telegrams. Write letters. And more than a hundred thousand letters to politicians by concerned individuals will produce more action than one statement by an organization, anyway.

As professionals, let's stay with our area of expertise. Let's make a difference in what we are trying to do in schools. Political activity is a siren's song that lures us away from our basic goal; it is an important after-school function, not our primary mission in life. Politics is central to us as citizens, but diverting to us as professionals.

# EDUCATION — PAST, PRESENT, FUTURE

## by George M. Thomas

*George M. Thomas, who assumed the office of Phi Delta Kappa international president in October 1995, is a professor at Mississippi State University in Meridian. He has been a teacher, counselor, school psychologist, special education project director, coach, and school administrator during his 30 years in education. George also has worked in several states, serving students from preschool through graduate school.*

Much has been written on the failures of public education in the last few years. Those of us in the profession have at times agreed and at other times been angered by these reports. Public opinion, according to the Phi Delta Kappa/Gallup Polls, varies from support of the local school to condemnation of schools in general. One fairly consistent belief of the public is that schools were "better" in the past and are failing the students today.

As we look to the future, we face both optimism and pessimism. To be a professional educator today is to live, as Dickens wrote, in "the best of times and the worst of times."

The future of education offers tremendous opportunities to respond to the needs and wants of a new society. Cultural changes that have occurred in the past will increase significantly in the future. The adage that it takes a whole village to raise a child is an indication of some of our trouble today, when we no longer have a village. The multicultural and divergent society of today and the future makes the two-parent, middle-class family with strong family, religious, education, and community values seem like a part of ancient history. Non-English-speaking, at-risk, and special needs children are a growing percentage of our school population. Our drug-infested and violent society affects the children who come to our schools. We cannot isolate ourselves

51

from our society, but must react to it if we are to meet the needs of our students. This calls for new systems of education. As Max DePree wrote, "We cannot become what we need to be by remaining what we are."

As our society becomes more multicultural, we face the problems of maintaining and accommodating diverse groups, but also of blending the diversity into a new whole. The question of balance between maintaining separate identities and blending together is a societal challenge in which the schools will play a major part. Do we maintain cultures or create a new culture? Do we become so consumed with maintaining that we forget to build and change, or do we become so consumed with building and change that we lose our past? And will we educators merely respond to social change or lead the way?

"Where there is no vision, the people will perish" is a concept from ancient history. In education we have a similar situation. If we do not plan for the future, we will see the education system perish. If we do not plan for the future, perhaps the education system *should* perish. Often, we spend so much time and energy protecting the past and preserving the present that we are not preparing for the future. Sometimes, the successes of the past and present contribute to our lack of progress. We become so comfortable with prior success that we resist change. But the world is changing, and to resist change will transform past success into future failure.

Our new society is not the segregated, family-value-based world of the 1940s; but we often administer our schools as if there has been no change. We bus children across town to schools that are operated as they were years ago. Our administrative systems and styles, buildings, curricula, and instructional methods have changed little. But the students come from a society that is drastically different.

In response, we tend to believe that running a school system for more hours each day and more days each year will "fix" the problems. We fail to see that if the system is having problems, the system itself must be changed, rather than changing only parts of the system or, worse, merely renaming the system. We must have reform, rather than retreat to the past; we must move out, rather than pull inward.

Technology provides tremendous opportunities for schools of today and tomorrow. Instant communication throughout the world removes the limitations of resource materials and sources of knowledge. Record keeping and paperwork that many teachers complain about can be handled by technology. Instructional methods using computers and virtual reality should become the norm for all students in the 21st century, rather than the privilege of select groups. Parents and students should be able to access instructional help and communicate from home to school readily and easily through improved technology.

As we move forward, the school must become a learning center for the community, rather than property surrounded by fences and declared off-limits after hours. Schools need to be open more hours and days throughout the year to accommodate the new society, rather than continuing to operate on the traditional agricultural model that has not changed since students had chores in the afternoon and farm work in the summer. Technology can link the community together so that we might re-establish some villages to help raise our children.

Technological innovations have always encountered resistance. Technology costs money, but it also demands that we alter our views. We treasured the manual typewriter, and many schools kept students from using the new electric typewriters because of the fear of a power failure. Some schools discouraged the use of calculators because the battery might run down and, besides, the students would not learn if machines did the work. Chalkboards and textbooks dominated instruction for years, while televisions and other new technology were kept in the library for "special" uses. Computer use was limited to the "expert" in the lab and to the business and mathematics departments. In driver education classes, we once did not allow the use of the new automatic transmission because we believed that everyone needed to master the clutch and manual transmission.

Today, many students own and use hand-held computers, carry cellular telephones in their pocket, use a fax machine at home, and drive or are driven to school in an automobile equipped with a phone, a CD player, a mapping system, and computerized electronic systems. Yet many schools are struggling still to make basic technology readily available to students and teachers.

As schools and societies change, educators also must change how they do their work. Lifelong learning for teachers must be a reality. New methods, materials, technology, systems, and programs will require a commitment to continuous growth and development. School systems will need to provide time and opportunities for the teachers to renew and retrain. The traditional staff development activities will give way to more useful and meaningful training. Distance learning, computers, and the Internet and the World Wide Web will provide opportunities never before available.

The traditional model of group training that requires physical attendance will continue because of the need for professional interaction, but it will be a minor part of the training. Professional materials will continue to be printed on paper and transmitted on video and voice tapes; but current electronic transmission methods will be expanded, and new methods will be developed. As we have come to expect and accept body-part transplants in the medical field, so we will develop a new method of information transfer between persons in education. In time, the school as we know it today may even cease to exist. Individuals living in the late 21st century may look back at our archaic system and wonder how a person ever became educated.

Teacher preparation, recruitment, and retention are concerns that must be dealt with today if education is to improve in the future. Colleges and universities are changing their teacher preparation programs; but in many instances, the changes are being made only in response to external pressure, rather than on perceived needs.

Similarly, an emphasis on material at the expense of method will not work. Teachers must know more about how students learn and how to teach. Too much time in the past has been spent on unrelated theoretical ideas. This must be changed to an application model of instruction and preparation. Emphasis will be on how to *think,* how to secure information and use it, and how to relate to a changing society. We have for too long used a model of memorization and recitation; with the increasing use of technology, the new emphasis will be on access and usage.

The role of the teacher was once a valued role in our society, but this no longer is so. In order to recruit persons into teaching, the teacher's valued role in society must be reasserted. Educators can work toward a better image by exercising more professional behavior and by working with the community, rather than blaming the community for the problems with which they must deal in their classrooms.

Equity in programs, services, funding, and facilities also is a problem that must be dealt with. No longer can we accept the idea that where people live will determine the quality of their education. We live in a mobile society; but many persons are place-bound, and this should not limit their opportunities to participate in quality education programs. Technology will help to equalize offerings, but we must do more. We must spend necessary funds to enhance opportunities for those who have suffered most from funding inequities of the past, such as rural and inner-city schools. Will we continue to depend on the federal government to solve these problems and accept their increased presence, or will we begin to deal with our problems in our communities, cities, and states?

Planning for excellence, change, and growth offers an opportunity for all concerned persons to become involved, for teachers, administrators, parents, students, and the larger community all to take a part in this endeavor. We must come together to develop goals, objectives, and strategies for the future based on a realistic assessment of our present condition combined with our vision for the future. Goals 2000 was an attempt, but the goals were too general and carried no built-in plan for implementation. As we develop a new plan, everyone who will be affected by the plan must be involved, not just a select group of politicians. For acceptance by all, we need involvement by all.

We can accomplish the changes we need and desire if we dedicate our efforts. Many persons say we must go back to the past in order to shape the future. However, true education professionals will lead the way and shape a future that responds to the changing realities of the present, rather than one that attempts to recapture a rosy, half-remembered past. We can have the future that we are willing to develop.

# HELP WANTED: EDUCATIONAL ENTREPRENEURS

by Donald P. Anderson

*Donald P. Anderson is dean emeritus of the College of Education at Ohio State University. Formerly a high school mathematics and physics teacher and a principal, he joined the OSU faculty in 1966 and served as dean for nine years, retiring in 1992. Don is president of a consulting firm, Educational Initiatives, Inc., and is a member of the Board of Governors of the Phi Delta Kappa Educational Foundation.*

One of the charges to authors in this collection was to predict changes in education into the 21st century based on their own experiences. I found that attempting to make such predictions to be a difficult task for two reasons. First, the rapid changes in technology, especially in the processing of information, afford a tremendous opportunity for change and set a compelling challenges for all who work in schools, who have responsibility for their governance, and who are concerned about education. The second reason relates to the recent relaxing of regulations or codes of practice in the public schools. The easing of instructional requirements has the potential to bring about significant change in the way schools go about their business. Together, these two changes form the major thesis of this essay.

The Industrial Age has been replaced by the Information Age. More information has been produced in the last 30 years than during the previous 5,000. The information supply available to us doubles every five years. In 1991, for the first time, companies spent more on computing and communication equipment than the combined amount spent on construction, industrial, mining, and farm equipment.* Schools no longer

---

*Price Pritchett, *New Work Habits for a Radically Changing World* (Dallas: Pritchett and Associates, 1994), p. 4.

57

can serve as information transmissions systems; the emphasis has to change to knowledge utilization.

All of this is happening when the new technology is exploding and the potential for changing the way instruction is delivered is greater than at any time since the invention of the printing press. We are at the crossroads in the evolution of schooling.

I began my career in education more than forty years ago. Five days after being given notice that the Air Force had too many junior officers, I was released from active duty and was on the job as a mathematics and science teacher in a small, rural high school in Minnesota. After two years teaching in that district and another two years in a suburban Minneapolis school system, I went back to that rural high school as its principal.

Being a teacher and administrator 40 years ago was quite different from performing those roles today. Educators generally were held in high regard by the parents and the larger community. Neither the students nor the parents were critical or very demanding of the schools. There was parental support for most actions that teachers took, including the handling of student discipline. Lawsuits against the schools were almost unheard of.

There were no elaborate curriculum guides. The textbooks, typically chosen by administrators with limited input from the teachers, guided the curriculum. Teachers were expected to "cover the material," and there was little if any press to raise college entrance examination grades.

What happened to change all this?

The tranquility of the past is gone. Many students, parents, and policy makers are voicing concerns about the schools — about teachers, administrators, and board members. They demand more accountability. They challenge educators' actions in the courts, in public meetings, and in the press.

A major reason for this change is the schools' success. We are, in fact, living with the "consequences of success." For years, educators have espoused the objective of developing critical thinking skills. And now, these critical thinkers, whom we prepared, are focusing their criticism on the schools, on all public and many private bodies, on public policy makers, and on professionals, including doctors, lawyers, and teachers. This new, more educated population expects more from the schools; and they are challenging the work of educators. Those comfortable days of the past are gone and will never return.

Employers also are making new and greater demands on the schools. No longer can students be prepared merely for jobs. They must be prepared for careers, because jobs are changing so rapidly. Employers are looking for persons who have good work habits, who can work in teams, and who are lifelong learners, in addition to having basic communication and computation skills.

National and state standards also are being proposed. State-mandated proficiency testing is sweeping across the country. Local, state, and national policy makers impose standards and constraints on the schools. State legislators respond to the accountability issue by mandating proficiency tests, many of which measure memory and recall. State education departments are pressed into designing curricula intended to set standards for student performance.

One of the most positive trends that has resulted from the school reform movement is shared decision making. The word *empowerment* has come into our vocabulary. Site-based management took some of the control from the central office and placed it in the hands of the principals and teachers. Teachers were empowered to have more control of their own actions. Parents and students also have pressed for empowerment.

Recently, I had the good fortune to observe some excellent teachers and administrators in action. I am hopeful that the movement toward empowering educators and other school stakeholders spreads. Empowerment broadens the "ownership" in schools and fosters positive risk taking.

When I interviewed a number of successful school principals, I asked them to identify their best teachers and to specify some of the characteristics these teachers have in common. Here are a few of their responses:

> She is passionate about teaching and working with her students. This passion for teaching and learning is infectious. Many of her students begin to share this passion for the subject she teaches and for learning in general.

> He is creative and a risk taker. He is not satisfied with using only the resources that we make available.

> Rather than whining about not getting all of the supplies and services she requests, she goes out and finds them.

> He uses the community — the organizations and the personnel — like no one I have ever seen before.

> They are not satisfied to confine their instruction to the classroom and the resources found in the school.

> They would make a fortune in the private sector; they truly are a bunch of entrepreneurs!

Two examples of such teachers follow. The first example portrays a group of teachers in a high school science department; the second focuses on a single high school social studies teacher.

A group of area high school science teachers have produced an extraordinary number of state science-fair winners. In three of the last six years, their students have earned composite ratings higher than any other secondary school in the state. In one of the other three years, their colleagues in the district's other high school captured that distinction. How have they done it?

For one thing, a former school board member is a professor of nuclear engineering at Ohio State University. Through him, they found ways for many of their students to spend time on campus, working with leading scientists and researchers and using laboratory equipment that the high school simply could not afford. They worked with university faculty members in developing proposals for funded research and development projects and used these faculty members, some of whom live in the community, as unpaid consultants.

With very limited resources from the school district, they turned a 14-acre pond on a edge of their school property into an excellent outdoor education facility. They sought and received funding to build an outdoor education building with a classroom and spaces for individual research and storage.

They also convinced their school board that funds should be available to support academic coaches, just as there are funds allocated for athletic coaches. These modest stipends for academic coaches kept the classrooms and laboratories open in the evenings and on weekends so that students could engage in their own research projects. These teachers also sought and received support from the administration and the board of education to remodel their classrooms to include stations for individual student research projects.

The second example is a social studies teacher in a suburban/rural high school. In spite of the fact that the school system has had a relatively poor financial base in the past, he has provided students with a wealth of experiences. This teacher sees the entire geographic region as a resource. Through his efforts to engage local citizens in a school project, a very active community historical society came into being. He has tapped a wide range of individuals and organizations in the community as resources for the classroom. His students engage in a variety of community projects. In fact, with the help of some of his students, he recently dismantled an old log cabin that was about to be demolished.

It will be rebuilt on the school site as part of his plans to create a small-scale pioneer village.

During the most recent presidential election campaign, he suggested to the principal that the entire secondary school staff and students get involved in a real-time learning situation. With the support of his colleagues and the principal, such election issues as the environment, family values, and economics formed the basis for a week-long curriculum. Regular classes were suspended for one day so that students could hold political conventions and campaign for their issues and candidates. At the conclusion of this project, students voted on a number of issues in addition to casting votes for their favorite presidential candidate.

What do the teachers identified in these examples have in common? Simply this: They take risks.

They challenge the way things have been done in the past. They seek out new resources to bring into the classroom. They build support among colleagues and administrators. *They behave as entrepreneurs.*

The time is right to unleash the potential of these entrepreneurial teachers and administrators. To make significant changes in a system once so constrained will require employing — and preparing — a new kind of school professional: the education entrepreneur.

Webster's New Collegiate Dictionary defines *entrepreneur* as one who organizes, manages, and assumes the risks of a business or enterprise. Usually we view entrepreneurs as individuals who can take an idea and pursue it largely by themselves. Some of the authors writing in this area make the distinction between an entrepreneur who operates alone and an *intrapreneur* who operates with and among colleagues inside a larger organization.

Education entrepreneurs (or intrapreneurs, because they almost always work in collaboration) bridge the gap between research and the marketplace. In some cases, they actually design a new product based on knowledge and research generated by others. In other cases, they find new and better ways to develop and market the product, emphasizing the development and marketing processes, not just the product itself. They are optimistic and exhibit trust in themselves and their colleagues. They have commitment to and faith in their ideas. Schools provide prime opportunities for entrepreneurial behavior.

Robert Hisrich* has identified the following aspects of an entrepreneurial environment:

---

*Robert Hisrich, *Entrepreneurship, Intrapreneurship, and Venture Capital* (Lexington, Mass.: Lexington Books, 1986), p. 77.

- The organization operates on the frontiers of technology.
- New ideas are encouraged.
- Trial and error is encouraged and failures are allowed.
- Approaches call for multidisciplinary teamwork.
- Goals are long-term.
- Volunteerism is encouraged.
- Appropriate rewards are provided.
- Sponsors and champions are available, and top management is supportive.

The schools possess most, if not all, of those aspects.

Looking to the future, it is very evident that schooling has to move rapidly beyond the information-transmission model of the past. The schools must focus on inquiry and lifelong learning, with increasing emphasis on multidisciplinary content. In the decades ahead, everyone will need to be able to collect, collate, and use information; and so teachers themselves must model lifelong learning. They must spend more time working as mentors and coaches than as lecturers and information transmitters. They must model critical thinking, problem solving, decision making, and risk taking.

To get these education entrepreneurs into the classrooms of tomorrow, today's leaders can take two approaches: First, we can attempt to recruit and train the entrepreneurs. Clearly, we can extend our recruiting pool for teacher education students. When Ohio State University moved its teacher training programs from the undergraduate level to the graduate level, very different kinds of persons applied and were admitted to the programs. Most had some work experiences in fields other than education, and many were parents. Many more minority students applied than had applied to the undergraduate program; they brought with them a refreshing set of insights and experiences.

A second approach is to release the current teaching staff from bureaucratic shackles. The entrepreneurial teachers described previously had one other important thing in common. They were working with building and district administrators who encouraged and supported them. Most education leaders realize that we lose a significant number of bright young teachers after only a few years in the classroom. Many of the brightest and most creative leave when boredom sets in; they cannot live with the isolation of being confined to a classroom hour after hour. They feel so constrained by working in an outdated system of education that they elect to leave the profession.

To change that environment and to provide a positive climate for risk taking, administrators must be visionary and flexible, create options, encourage teamwork and open discussion, build a coalition of supporters, and be supportive and persistent. Entrepreneurial teachers cannot operate unless the climate is right.

It is the responsibility of building and district leadership, who themselves must be entrepreneurs, to set the stage. These leaders must understand the climate and culture of the school community. They must protect the teachers who are designing and implementing new systems or strategies. They must view schools as laboratories where ideas are tested and evaluated. They must accept failure, learn from it, and act on what is learned. Just as in business, failures or losses have to be considered as investments and something to learn from. If these new strategies appear to be moving beyond community norms, the support of students, parents, and other community members must be cultivated. The community must be fully engaged in the schools and a level of trust established before moving ahead.

The combination of new technology and the reduction in bureaucratic constraints provides opportunities to create schools that will meet our future needs. And only by creating such schools now can we attract to the profession of education those young entrepreneurs who can ensure that future students will receive an education worthy of their high potential.

# ENHANCING THE PRESENCE OF AFRICAN-AMERICAN TEACHERS

by Howard D. Hill

*Howard D. Hill is director of chapter programs for Phi Delta Kappa, a position he has held since 1987. He also is an adjunct professor of Afro-American Studies at Indiana University. Prior to moving to Bloomington, Indiana, Howard was professor of education and chair of the Department of Teacher Education at South Carolina State University in Orangeburg.*

During the past 25 years, the United States has witnessed a serious decline in the presence of African Americans in education across the nation. Veteran African-American educators anxiously await the time that they can retire from the profession, and the younger generations seem to disdain the profession that many black Americans once held dear. Although there are other factors, nine in particular directly contribute to the decline of African Americans in teaching:

1. More favorable job opportunities for African Americans are now available.
2. Teaching is perceived by younger African Americans to be a low-status profession.
3. Salaries in education are less attractive when compared to those in numerous other professions.
4. Teaching has become a relatively dangerous profession with a proliferation of violence in the schools. (The 26th Annual Phi Delta Kappa/Gallup Poll of the Public's Attitudes Towards the Public Schools finds that, for the first time ever, the category "fighting, violence, and gangs" shares the number-one position with "lack of discipline" as the greatest problem confronting local public schools.)

5. State regulatory policies and entry-level testing now block a relatively large percentage of prospective African Americans from choosing teaching as a career.
6. Today's students are much more difficult to teach; some seem to not want to study and learn. Some African-American students feel they are "acting white" if they excel in the classroom.
7. The field of education has become a profession where professional esteem and recognition are hard to come by.
8. Education was very cruel to African Americans with the advent of school integration in the South in the 1960s.
9. There is a perceived lack of support from parents and guardians regarding their children's education.

Few experiences are more disheartening than visiting schools where there are more African-American students (and other minorities) than white students, but the majority of their teachers, counselors, school support personnel — and often the principals — are white. It is even more disheartening that these schools usually are located in neighborhoods and communities where a majority of residents are African Americans and other minorities. African Americans, at one time, were highly visible in such schools. But where are the black educators now?

About 30 years ago, minorities collectively constituted 16% of the teaching force. But the winds of change that blew from the 1954 *Brown* v. *Topeka Board of Education* decision lowered this percentage, particularly that portion made up of African-American educators. The court said in the *Brown* decision, "In the field of public education the doctrine of 'separate and equal' has no place. Separate educational facilities are inherently unequal."[1] The National Education Association reported in 1974 that more than 30,000 African-American teachers lost their jobs in 17 Southern and border states in the 20 years since that 1954 Supreme Court decision. Thus, from the standpoint of African Americans in education, that decision dealt a serious, albeit unintended, blow.

The *Swann* v. *Charlotte-Mecklenburg* (North Carolina) *Board of Education* case was decided in 1971. This U.S. Supreme Court decision stated that involuntary busing was a legitimate means of achieving racial integration in the schools. The implications of this decision were that 1) de facto segregation in northern urban school districts would come under close scrutiny of the courts, and 2) busing would be considered a legitimate tool for implementing school desegregation plans. The court ruled that traditional arguments about the value of neighborhood schools could no longer be used to avoid integration; now school districts would be viewed as unitary systems; and whenever possible, racial integration within those districts would be achieved.[2]

With the *Brown* decision mandating school integration and the *Swann* decision insisting that involuntary busing was a legitimate means of achieving school integration, the careers of black teachers and administrators were drastically altered. Thousands of black students were encouraged to use freedom of choice plans to attend predominantly white schools. Although these transfers were relatively small compared to the number of students that might have participated in them, this exodus of students set in motion what would later become the consolidation of schools. Accompanying the consolidation of the schools was a "surplus" of educators, namely black principals, thousands of black teachers, and the few black superintendents there were.

Black career educators in the 1970s faced career consequences unforeseen prior to the *Brown* decision in 1954 and the subsequent movement to integrate America's schools. Persistently releasing black educators since school integration began, in my estimation, is the single most important cause of the decline of African-American teachers from approximately 12% of the teaching force to the present 8%.[3]

Howard Hodgkinson, the respected demographer, has predicted that by the year 2000, the presence of blacks in teaching will be approximately 5%. This will occur at a time when blacks and other minority group members will constitute a majority of the student population in many urban school districts. Indeed, by 2000, one-third of the nation's students will be minorities.

I predict that we will not see that 5% low. Now under way are aggressive efforts to encourage minorities — blacks in particular — to seek careers in teaching and education administration. Colleges and universities, professional associations in education, government, etc., are developing strategies and initiatives designed to shore up the population of ethnic and racial minorities in the teaching profession. They will succeed!

## Strength in Diversity

The United States serves a diverse, multicultural school population. In cities in all 50 states, dozens of familial, linguistic, and cultural patterns are evident in schools. For these reasons, among others, a societal imperative must be to develop programs and information outlets that assist in the recruitment, preparation, and placement of prospective minority educators.

The school also must, of necessity, diversify its experiences. And minority educators will have to take the lead in building cultural bridges when conflicts arise over ethnic, racial, or socio-educational problems. These educators and their use of effective communication tools, their interpretation of customs, traditions, beliefs, and other sociocultural influences under their control, are needed to help students in general, but minority students in particular, to succeed at school and in life.

Research by Geneva Gay and other social policy experts strongly encourages educators to diversify their ranks by employing school personnel who reflect the multicultural nature of society. This goal stems from the belief that America's strength lies in its diversity, and much needs to be done to make certain that education both meets the needs and enriches the experiences of all students.[4] As Gonzalo Ramirez, a school administrator in Texas, once said to me, "The degree to which multicultural education becomes a reality in our schools depends largely upon the attitudes and behaviors of classroom teachers."

In this regard, it is contradictory for African Americans to insist that the schools reflect the pluralistic nature of society while, at the same time, they make only marginal contributions to the pool of educators. African Americans have been in the teaching profession since 1744; and minority students profit from firsthand experiences with successful, professional role models. Non-minority students also gain a clearer, more accurate understanding of our diverse general population through their close interaction with authority figures from different cultures. And students who participate in harmonious, productive, cross-cultural relationships in the classroom are better prepared to succeed in a culturally diverse work environment.

We know that only by strengthening the presence of African Americans and other non-whites in schools will we achieve that necessary strength through diversity that is essential for America's schools to serve all their constituents. Thus it is incumbent on African Americans to work to increase their professional presence in education. This is a situation that is directly under their control in the quest to have the teaching force reflect the plurality of the nation.

It is conceivable that African Americans can regain the ground they lost in education during the 1960-1980 period when many were summarily and systematically squeezed out of the profession. For a start, the goal for African-American participation in education by the year 2005 should be no lower than 15% of the national teaching force. This is a goal that African Americans can use to demonstrate their capacity to influence the preparation, placement, and retention of African-American educators.

## Leading with Vision and Determination

The historically black colleges and universities (HBCUs) are the institutions that initially supplied the nation with its African-American teachers. These institutions included the Hampton Normal and Agricultural Institute, Tuskegee Institute, Cheney (Pennsylvania) University, Wilberforce (Ohio) College, and Lincoln (Pennsylvania) University. These were a few of the schools established by blacks in their effort toward self-education. In the area of teacher preparation, these HBCUs, and others developed after them (there are now 117), have served and continue to fulfill their mission well in the preparation of non-white educators.

With the advent of school integration in the 1950s and the displacement of African-American educators in the 1960s and 1970s, HBCUs began to sense that teacher preparation programs were falling into disfavor with their enrollees. Unlike their counterparts at the predominantly white institutions, some HBCUs began to de-emphasize or shift their program emphasis from education to such fields as engineering, the health professions, business, the social sciences, and the liberal arts. The institutions saw little reason to maintain education programs with dwindling enrollments. Compounded by the uncertainly of the education job market for African Americans, the decline in the number of teacher preparation programs at HBCUs is understandable.

If African Americans are to reclaim a significant place in the teaching profession, a leading force will need to be the National Association for Equal Opportunity in Higher Education (NAFEO) and the historically black institutions of higher education that maintained their teacher education programs. This is not to imply that UCLA, George Peabody College for Teachers, Michigan State University, University of Tulsa, Northern Colorado University, Indiana University, Rutgers University, University of Florida, Brigham Young University, DePaul University, and other outstanding schools will not have a hand in supplying the nation with capable African-American teachers. Rather, I simply mean that the HBCUs have the traditional edge in supplying the nation with educators of color. They must lead with vision and determination in supplying the nation with high-quality minority teachers.

Former U.S. Supreme Court Justice Oliver Wendell Holmes once said, "The greatest thing in the world is not so much where we are, but in what direction we are moving." There are ample reasons for educators and policy makers to feel the corner has been turned regarding the number of African-American students in teacher preparation programs.

First of all, students are returning in great numbers to education programs. Second, there is evidence of quality education majors (those fully admitted to teacher education programs) being reported from South Carolina State University, Grambling State University, Prairie View A&M University, Delaware State University, Le Moyne-Owen College, Clark Atlanta University, Tuskegee University, Philander Smith College, North Carolina A&T University, Florida A&M University, North Carolina Central University, and others. These are just a few of the HBCUs with prominent teacher education programs. And third, the HBCUs have a strength that goes beyond tradition on predominantly white campuses: They possess the largest collective percentage of African-American students from which to attract teacher education majors.

However, if the HBCUs are to achieve success in attracting and preparing contemporary African-American educators, they must shape their vision and determination around the following 10 goals:

1. To work with public school personnel and community leaders to increase the pool of students eligible to attend college. The larger the pool of students, the greater the percentage of students likely to major in teacher education. It is definitely in the best interest of all HBCUs with teacher education programs to develop affiliations with the various future teacher organizations that exist across the country.

2. To imbue African-American students in all divisions at the HBCUs with a notion that teaching is a desirable career choice. Students also need to know that a degree in teaching leads to other attractive career choices: school administration, education consulting, and so on. Because many freshman and sophomore students have not decided on major fields of study and can benefit from being steered toward a teaching career, encourage them to seek a career in education.

3. To give priority to teacher education programs at HBCUs as never before. It is not enough for a college president or chancellor merely to talk about the importance of a department of education. Sufficient funding, professional staff, student support services, and facilities must be provided for the programs. Although teacher education is expensive, it is the one department the institution cannot afford to be without.

4. To devise creative ways 1) to attract the support of educators and major corporations that are willing to work with HBCU teacher education programs and their special mission, 2) to build endowment programs for teacher education, 3) to collaborate with other institutions interested in developing alliances to improve teacher education, and 4) to solicit alumni for program support, assistance with student recruit-

ment, program enhancement, and public relations that emphasize the success HBCUs have experienced in preparing teachers and administrators.

5. To diversify the student ranks at the HBCUs. Some HBCUs in recent years have experienced relatively large enrollment gains of Caucasian students. (*Black Issues in Higher Education* recently reported that white student enrollment at the nation's HBCUs increased by 111%, or 10,388 students, between 1976 and 1990.) Caucasians and students of other races provide HBCUs with the opportunity to prepare students of different racial backgrounds for careers teaching in racially, culturally, and ethnically diverse situations. It would be to the advantage of white students, particularly those who anticipate teaching in urban schools, to matriculate for their initial degrees (bachelors and masters) at the HBCUs.

6. To develop a specialized cadre of instructors and professors with responsibilities in teaching, research, and service geared mainly toward teacher education programs. These professionals must be expected to 1) recruit eligible students to the teacher education programs, 2) provide counseling and guidance to their advisees, 3) serve on curriculum planning committees, 4) develop and execute well-planned instruction, 5) prepare proposals for external funding, 6) present papers on teacher preparation at conferences and conventions, and 7) engage in timely visits to public, private, and parochial schools for firsthand professional renewal.

7. To provide systematic group study and remediation activities for students whose success in college has been less than satisfactory. To assist these students with the completion of their degree requirements, professors and advisors will need to help these students learn how to study more effectively and to overcome test anxiety. Ample resources are available for educators to assist prospective teachers in this area. Educators must possess the will to succeed.

8. To recruit students to teaching based on specialty areas (math education, science education, special education, social studies education, language arts and reading, etc.) rather than on their ethnic or racial background. Colleges and universities must elevate their student recruitment efforts to emphasize program offerings and the quality of faculty they possess. Strong teachers emerge from programs with high-quality professors.

9. To monitor teacher education programs at HBCUs diligently by maintaining the high standards set for education by state, regional, and national accreditation bodies. HBCUs should strive to exceed the standards — to be recognized by their peer institutions as leaders in the

excellence of their teacher preparation programs. Excellent programs have school personnel officers camping out at the institutions and seeking the services of their graduates.

10. To develop faith and pride in what could be called the era of resurgent teacher education programs at HBCUs. HBCUs met the challenge of preparing African-American teachers during the eras of extreme segregation in the American society. They possess the potential to address the current shortage of African-American educators. It appears that many of them have the resolve to meet the minority teacher shortage head on.

## Marketing Teacher Education

There are as many ways to market education to African Americans as there are available marketing strategies. No one strategy has a marked advantage over any other. The important thing is that organizations carrying out teacher recruitment efforts through coalitions must reach the consciousness of African Americans with impact — through creative and innovative approaches. African Americans realize that there is a shortage of teachers, but many regard the teacher shortage as insignificant. They need to be made to feel the need to solve the shortage.

An essential, creative, and innovative marketing approach is the use of coalitions. African Americans can be convinced through the sincere influence of "significant" others that the minority teacher recruitment efforts are central to their social, economic, and political well-being. In managing student recruitment efforts for successful outcomes, I recommend the following strategies:

*Identify allies and common interests.* Look beyond the traditional allies (churches, education associations, the state department of education, etc.) for support. Seek the support of the local Chamber of Commerce, black fraternities and sororities, Jack and Jill of America, the Links, NAACP, Urban League, barbers, cosmetologists, radio and television stations, and other groups that attract broad followings. There are students — the young and nontraditional — waiting to be invited to education.

But be prepared for some black middle-class families to counter the efforts of HBCUs to expand their teacher education mission. It is not uncommon for teachers, administrators, and guidance counselors to encourage "bright" young people not to major in teacher education and to steer them toward the more lucrative or prestigious professions. And employment statistics do show that talented and ambitious African Americans are heading for other career fields.

*Clearly identify the problem.* Devote time, attention, and resources to recruitment efforts. A half-hearted effort will produce minimal gains. Conduct continuous research to determine the major and sub-issues in the anticipated recruitment drive. To reach the pulse of contemporary African-American youngsters and nontraditional students, HBCUs must conduct constant and reliable research to determine the prospective students' likes and dislikes about the teaching profession. Today's students want to know they are needed to be more than role models or just to increase the percentage of educators of color for statistical purposes.

*Target recruitment campaigns, using print and nonprint media to highlight the importance of education as a career of choice.* Use color and contemporary imagery to highlight the historical and contemporary contributions of blacks in education. Prepare different campaign materials for various audiences. Target high schools with high percentages of black students with appropriate brochures, videos, etc.

*Develop graduate degree programs devoted to excellence in education.* Offer symposia, forums, and special experiences that relate to the development of the contemporary educator. Also, develop statewide networks for school counselors. School counselors and their perception of the quality of institutions of higher education can impede or advance the amount of influence an HBCU has on education.

*Provide meaningful scholarships and fellowships for persons pursuing degrees and certificates in education.* Early financial recognition engenders greater respect for the profession of education. Scholarships and fellowships also convey the message that financial incentives for educators are available.

*Start Future Educators of America organizations in the local schools.* Black students can be taught through clubs the importance of teaching as a career. FEA clubs may be organized by contacting Phi Delta Kappa International Headquarters in Bloomington, Indiana.

## The PDK and NABSE Alliance

HBCUs must take the leadership role in supplying African-American educators for the nation's schools, but other organizations also can play a role in this effort. Recently, an alliance was formed between Phi Delta Kappa and the National Alliance of Black School Educators

(NABSE) to complement the efforts of HBCUs and other organizations that have programs dedicated to building a diverse teaching force.

Phi Delta Kappa is a white-majority professional organization that at one time restricted its membership to white men; it opened its ranks to blacks in the 1940s and to women in the 1970s. NABSE is an organization that serves as an advocate for the interests of African Americans. However, there are white educators in its membership. Although the two organizations pursue different interests in education, they have common goals in the recruitment of future educators.

Since the NABSE/PDK Alliance was formed in 1994, Recruiting New Teachers (RNT) and the U.S. Department of Education have met with the two organizations to formulate plans for a national conference designed to enhance the presence of under-represented groups in the teaching profession. Representatives of the four organizations laid the groundwork for a national conference, titled "Recruiting Persons of Color to Teaching."

Several goals were outlined for the conference, including sharing what is known about effective strategies for diversifying the teaching force and determining what educators still need to know to reach desirable outcomes. Conference planners developed an action plan that is to be implemented by organizations participating in the event. Representatives of national organizations that are active in efforts to diversify the teaching force met to develop the specific agenda for educators to consider. The planners anticipate inviting about 125 participants, representing organizations with a strong interest in the topic. Synthesis papers from the conference will be published to ensure a wide dissemination of the information and strategies designed to enhance the presence of people of color in education.

The national PDK/NABSE conference could be the beginning of what should be a fruitful collaboration between two professional organizations that stand united in the common goal to have a broader ethnic and racial representation in the education profession. The alliance between PDK and NABSE is the kind of leverage organizations can use to enhance the presence of under-represented groups in education, particularly African Americans.

## Individual Initiatives

Finally, I believe it is important to encourage individuals and families to take personal initiatives to support minority recruitment to teaching. For example, when an alumnus underwrites a $1,000 annually renewable scholarship for an African-American student who 1) has been admitted to the teacher education program and 2) is a college junior, that individual donor affects not just the single student who receives the scholarship. The donor also sets a pattern that may be replicated by other donors and at other institutions.

I have taken this initiative personally, in a small effort to help increase the percentage of African Americans in the education programs at Arkansas State University, where I earned a master's degree. If this small gesture were replicated by individuals across the United States, those funds would complement the larger scholarships and fellowships provided by colleges, universities, corporations, and government sources.

Individual donors gain satisfaction from the act of giving, and there are tangible tax benefits as well. But more important is that small scholarships serve to encourage recipients and to sustain their interest in an education career far out of proportion to the actual monetary award.

## Concluding Thoughts

The best recommendation that I have heard for increasing the percentage of African Americans in teaching was offered by Barbara Hatton, the president of South Carolina State University in Orangeburg, when she spoke at the 42nd Biennial Council of Phi Delta Kappa, which was held in St. Louis in 1989. She said, "Increase the pool of students who graduate from high school. From this expanded group of students will come a large percentage that may view teaching favorably, wish to serve as role models for students of color, and wish to make contributions to society via the profession." As communities become more involved in preschool programs and Head Start, students will be more likely to graduate; and the ripple effect will be felt at the other end.

But there is an immediate need that we can — and must — address now. The percentage of African-American teachers is too low. Unless we take steps now to recruit more African Americans to teaching, that percentage will continue to shrink. In a nation where minorities, collectively, are becoming the majority in many cities, allowing this dwindling of African-American educators to continue would be disastrous.

More important, African Americans have much to offer as teachers, not merely to children of color but to children of all colors. Our diverse nation needs equally diverse schools — diverse students, diverse teachers, diverse administrators.

Phi Delta Kappa's *2000 and Beyond* statement captures the spirit of teaching well:

> Education is a noble cause and calling. Schools are established for society, and every society wants the best — the very best — for its own youth. Those who choose to serve their fellow human beings by working with students and others in schools assume an important responsibility: A commitment to help others become different, better people through the use of intelligence rather than power, through persuasion rather than coercion, through knowledge rather than intimidation or deceit.

In summary, three recommendations are advanced for enhancing the presence of African-American teachers. First, HBCUs must lead the way in supplying teachers of African-American ancestry to the schools. Second, national alliances, akin to the PDK/NABSE consortium, must be started. Third, personal and financial incentives, supported by organizations and individuals, must be aimed at talented individuals.

African Americans themselves, currently the largest minority group in the United States, must possess a greater will to return to the profession they have served so well. They hold the power to allow the shortage of African Americans in education to continue or to change the equation. Education is indeed a noble cause and calling, and the tremendous talents of African Americans are needed.

## Footnotes

1. James A. Banks, "Race, Ethnicity, and School in the United States: Past, Present, and Future," in *Multicultural Education in Western Societies*, edited by James A. Banks and James Lynch (New York: Praeger, 1986), p. 38.
2. Kern M. Alexander and M. David Alexander, *American Public School Law* (New York: West, 1985), pp. 433-41.
3. Center for Educational Statistics, *Racial Makeup of the Teaching Force* (Washington, D.C.: U.S. Department of Education, 1992).
4. Geneva Gay, "Multicultural Teacher Education," in *Multicultural Education in Western Societies*, edited by James A. Banks and James Lynch (New York: Praeger, 1986), pp. 154-77.

# CAN EDUCATORS GIVE UP CONTROL OF LEARNING?

## by Douglas Bedient

*Douglas Bedient served as the international president of Phi Delta Kappa from 1993 until 1995. He is a professor of curriculum and instruction at Southern Illinois University at Carbondale, where he has been employed since 1969. Doug previously was a social studies teacher in Green River, Wyoming.*

Critics sometimes charge that education is the only part of current life that George Washington, Thomas Jefferson, or other famous historical personalities would recognize should they be reincarnated and visit our modem society. Sadly, they might be right.

Transportation has progressed from the horse and buggy to space-age automobiles, and the idea of flying would boggle the minds of George and Tom. They might recognize today's ships and tankers, but their power and size have changed so dramatically that they would be astounded. The economy has changed from the agrarian base that they knew through an industrial period and now to the Information Age. They would be totally lost in front of a computer.

Medicine would be a happy revelation to George, with all his "wooden teeth" problems. And modern pharmaceuticals would seem strange compared to the leeches that were used in his day to treat illness by eliminating so-called bad blood.

But have the schools changed?

Washington and Jefferson were accustomed to schools where a group of students met with a teacher and the classroom was the domain for most school learning. Jefferson's beloved University of Virginia was similarly equipped for instruction. Materials were available in the library. While the resources are much more plentiful, our first and third U.S. Presidents would be comfortable with the books and journals that form much of the resource collection in school, college, and university libraries.

In the 1700s, when Washington and Jefferson were students, the lecture was in fashion, just as it had been when Plato was meeting with students in Athens. And the idea of the teacher passing information to students through lectures and presentations thrives today. I often walk the halls of buildings on my own campus, as well as campuses where I visit, and fear that George and Tom would indeed recognize and feel quite comfortable in those settings.

Usually I observe one instructor at or near the front of the class and students sitting and listening to the presentation. Research indicates that the lecture is the preferred instructional method for professors. When students are given the opportunity to develop a lesson, one of the most favored is the introductory lecture. There is something about lecturing that is vitally important to teachers.

But sometimes the situation can become ludicrous. I remember passing one class where the instructor's voice boomed out of the lecture hall so emphatically that I wondered what was going on. I peeked in and was astounded to see the instructor at the front of the hall animatedly working his way through what was an impressive lecture. But the hall was nearly empty. Fewer than 10 students were spread around the huge room. I shook my head as I walked on and wondered why the class was not approached in some other fashion, given the small number of students and the huge room. We teachers often lament the opportunity to work with small groups or individual students. Here was an opportunity missed.

I find that student teachers are well indoctrinated in the importance of lectures. When I suggest an observation should be conducted, a typical reply often is, "Well, I won't be lecturing that day." Few students believe that tutoring, lab teaching, demonstrations, debates, simulations, or other techniques provide a basis for observation of teaching. Where did this infatuation with lecture as the instructional method come from? And how do we get rid of it?

In Washington and Jefferson's day, books were precious. Indeed, the invention of moveable type in the 1400s did not revolutionize education until paper became common and low-priced. Even today, some societies might require more lecture because printed materials are difficult to acquire. When I worked with a radio-based education program for Nepal, a major challenge was how to produce student materials, because paper is a luxury in that country. The logistics of radios, batteries, and broadcasting programs were easier to handle than the handouts or workbooks that required paper. But ours is a rich society where paper and printed materials are everywhere.

I tend to believe that the lecture thrives as a teaching method because the instructor has control. Lectures can be scripted to a level where timing is very predictable. The major topics can be identified and establish the route that will be taken to learn material. Lectures provide a way for faculty members to incorporate their own recent reading, study, and research into their presentations.

During a lecture the teacher can control how students are involved. Rhetorical questions can be posed and answered. What could be more predictable? Questions that are easy to handle can be presented to students, and the presentation can conclude by responding to these predetermined queries. If the agenda for the class is full, there is very limited opportunity to deal with the interests or concerns of students. Most learners are somewhat reluctant to break into a presentation and pose the questions that they find intriguing. These features of the lecture are useful if one wants to establish an agenda and avoid some of the pitfalls that may occur when interaction with students begins.

As the world progresses and more and more resources are available to students and teachers, our methods must change. Instead of determining what resources will be studied, we must find learners who are technologically competent and who identify resources that are current and relevant to the class. This change will force us to evaluate how we work with learners so that we can break away from the lecture as the predominant method of instruction. The wealth of resources may force us to become learners along with our students in ways we have not experienced before.

I would like to see a time when, if Washington and Jefferson were to visit a university classroom, they might wonder what was happening.

# THE STRUGGLE FOR THE SURVIVAL OF THE COMMON SCHOOL

## by David L. Clark

*David L. Clark is Kenan Professor of Education in the Program in Educational Leadership at the University of North Carolina at Chapel Hill. His research and writing have dealt with issues in federal policy in education and organizational theory. Recently, his focus has turned to current efforts to reform American education. He is a co-author with Terry Astuto and others of* Roots of Reform: Challenging the Assumptions that Control Change in Education *(PDK, 1994).*

The past four decades span my career in the field of education. Within that relatively brief period, to the everlasting credit of the American citizenry, children and youth who previously had fallen outside the commitment to common educational opportunity and access have become recognized legally and actually in American schools. Race and ethnicity are no longer justification for exclusion. Disabled children now are served in public school classrooms. Girls and young women no longer exist on the periphery of the classroom, often to be counseled away from serious academic work. The major accomplishment of American public schools in the second half of this century is that fewer children are invisible. As a matter of sustained public policy, the common school finally has been asserted to be the guiding principle of American education.

The American public school system is foremost among education systems in the world, not because it solves all the problems of America's children and youth, but because it tackles those problems. And it does so for all children, not just the privileged few. Regardless of race, ethnicity, gender, or handicapping condition, they are sought out and brought together in an environment of care and hope. If some children progress more slowly than others, the public school still continues to offer opportunities, still attempts to work with them as members of the school family. With limited resources and contact hours, the common school remains the best hope available to us as citizens to ensure a positive future for all children.

However, at the threshold of the millennium neither educators nor the general public are celebrating the achievements of the public schools. To the contrary, dissatisfaction with the schools chips away at the citizenry's confidence in the common school. Critics repeatedly challenge the performance of the schools on the basis of international comparisons of student achievement. Politicians and business leaders purport that the schools share the blame for America's failures in economic competition in the world market. The social, moral, and family problems afflicting our society are routinely blamed on deficiencies of the schools.

Sporadic attempts to refute such allegations with data are virtually ignored by the public media. Positive parent responses to the schools that their youngsters attend — responses that are tracked and reported yearly by the Phi Delta Kappa/Gallup polls — fall on deaf ears. Public education has been under unremitting attack for the past 15 years.

No organization or agency, public or private, can withstand negative criticism indefinitely. At this point in the maturation of the common school, when we should be celebrating the achievement of universal educational access, public education is, instead, confronted by high-pressure, persistent attacks on its very existence.

Now is a time to look back at what has been achieved in American education during the second half of this century and at where our efforts have fallen short of acceptable performance. In large measure, the signal achievement of American education in the past 50 years has been inclusion. This is no mean accomplishment if one believes, as I do, in Lawrence Cremin's elegantly argued thesis that "the genius of American education — its animating spirit, its most distinctive quality — lies in the commitment to popularization."[1]

On the other hand, the most unsettling evidence of ineffectiveness in the same period has been the public schools' failure to interrupt the relationship between the socioeconomic status of a child's family and the subsequent achievement of that child in school. Whatever reasons or excuses can be offered for this persistent condition, the hope of the common school — its commitment to popularization — will not be attained until this chain of failure is broken. The promised land for the "have nots" in this country is the possibility that the next generation of adults will be able to achieve what seems impossible for the current generation to attain.

The central challenge confronting us as a society at the millennium is to reduce the now-increasing gap between the advantaged and the disadvantaged among us. The common school, public education for all, is a tool to that end. That this tool needs to be honed more effectively to that purpose does not justify discarding the tool.

However, there are those who believe that other tools, other policies, would be better suited to the solution. Those most pessimistic among us are simply willing to give up. This position led New York Mayor Rudolph Giuliani to question whether education dollars should be spent "on every single young person, irrespective of that person's ability to learn? . . . Or do we spend on those who show some ability to be able to function better."[2] If you cannot answer that question without hesitation, then the common school is not for you. And over the past two decades this question has become an issue that is considered debatable by reasonable persons in our society. Shlomo Maital, a professor of Economics and Management at the Israel Institute of Technology in Haifa, regards such thinking as dominant in the United States of 1995: "America is a rich country that acts as if it were poor. It pretends it cannot afford to look after the poor, the sick, the handicapped, the underprivileged, the homeless, the immigrants. . . . America, it seems, has simplified its social and economic life down to a single goal: money."[3]

Whether or not Professor Maital has accurately captured the dominant mood of the American electorate is debatable. However, this view cannot be allowed to dominate education policy in the 21st century. The result of such a policy stance will be to widen the gap between the rich and the poor, which ultimately will destroy the fabric of our society. The United States already has proceeded too far down this route. The Children's Defense Fund reported that in 1992, "the share of all family income received by the poorest one-fifth of families shrank to 4.4% — the lowest since records began in 1947 — while the share going to the wealthiest one-fifth hit 44.6%, a record high."[4] Shockingly, the poverty rate increases as age decreases. While the poverty rate for adults in the United States is under 15%, the rate for children under six is 25%, and under three is 27%. This is no time to abandon public education.

Giving up on the public schools assumes many policy forms. The proposal that would lead to the most devastating effects on American public schools would be the adoption of national or state voucher plans. Supporters of vouchers believe that good old-fashioned competition will result in a combination private/public school pattern that will best serve all children. Not a chance! Children of poverty will be left behind in the "old system" while voucher schools are flooded with children of privilege. Privatization through vouchers will bring the same level of open access to services for the poor that currently is exhibited in our privatized health care system. Members of poverty-burdened households tend to stay in their own neighborhoods in cities. Alternative private schools located in and outside local neighborhoods eventually will become a talent drain, taking away the most able students through entry and retention policies. This result already troubles public school systems that are pursuing reform through magnet schools, charter schools, test schools, and other alternative techniques. In spite of efforts to balance entrants to such schools by ethnicity, gender, and socioeconomic status, neighborhood schools that once were diverse and viable now are overwhelmed by the proportion of low-performing and troubled youngsters in their student populations.

The underlying policy issue is being avoided by retreating to such compromise solutions to the problems now faced by public schools. All children will not be served by such policies. American public schools are not failing because they have embraced the concept of the common school. They are, in fact, not "failing" in any sense that could not be applied to our law enforcement, social service, health, or drug-prevention systems. The schools (at least open, public schools) always have and always will reflect the accomplishments and the failures of society as a whole. When the American family becomes less stable, the effects are felt in public school classrooms. When children live in poverty, their health, nutrition, and emotional problems come to school with them. When increasing numbers of families and children are homeless, the consequences of fear, despair, and uncertainty walk through the school doors with the students. When children and youth are daily exposed to violence, crime, and a drug culture, then crime and violence and drug use come into schools. The American common school *is* America — a reflection of the best and the worst of our times. We will only defer and deflect the problems faced by our school-age children and youth by running away from the only sensible path we can follow, which is to set about improving *all* schools for *all* students.

Frank Smith captured the essence of this argument in a recent *Kappan* article when he noted, "The trouble with the endless concern over 'problems' in education is that many well-meaning but often misguided and sometimes meddlesome people believe that solutions must exist. They waste their own and other people's time and energy trying to find and implement these solutions."[5] He believes, as I do, that the rash of well-meaning solutions from state-level assessment plans to mandated forms of instruction and bodies of content miss the point. Schools have to *do better* in the day-to-day contact between teachers and students. Teachers need to be supported and encouraged in their everyday interactions with students. Schools need more resources, space, and elbow room to do better. Smith argues that, "The education system may not be amenable to change — but people are."[6]

This challenge must be our starting point. The problems confronting our schools are endemic to this age in our society. We cannot run away from them or solve them by creating endless new gimmicks that obfuscate the real issues. The central reality faced by American public schools today is the increasing number of students entering the schools who do not have support systems adequate to protect them from hunger, danger, and despair. We must finally pay attention to those child advocates who, year after year, point out to us the incredible costs of child poverty — hunger and malnutrition, violence, inadequate health care, adolescent pregnancy, deficient housing, and homelessness. No more data need to be gathered. The picture has been clear for a decade. If we do not invest in the total lives of children and youth, it is pointless to invest in schools. Every state and every community must demand a significantly increased investment in the total lives of children and youth. If we do not succeed, the so-called failure of our public schools will continue to be cited as a convenient excuse to avoid our responsibility to protect, nurture, and cherish all the children of this country.

We need to begin at the beginning. Our most vulnerable young citizens are preschoolers. The overall rate of poverty among these infants and toddlers is 27%. The Hispanic Development Project reported that 40% of Hispanic children under age six were living in poverty. Sharon Kagan captures this imperative clearly:

> Changes in the nation's demography, coupled with changes in our knowledge about the efficacy of early care and education, have generated the need to convert what has been a piecemeal, episodic approach to the construction of early childhood social policy into a new normative system for children in America. Such a system . . . must be so universal and so regularized (without being compulsory) that participation in it will be as natural and unstigmatized for all populations as is participation in our education system.[7]

Of course, our public schools need to change to meet the changing population that will become the majority population in the public schools in the 21st century. Such changes, supported by a sensible public investment in preschool education and early childhood services, also will involve increased expenditure of public funds. Diverse populations of learners need diverse programs of study and individual attention to effectively include those students in the school community. The students need to succeed daily, not just on year-end tests. They need adult role models who care for them and care about their problems and successes. They need teachers who understand them and who have the time and commitment to work out individual solutions to daily problems. They will need schools that are routinely small (the new Carnegie Report suggests elementary schools of 300 to 500 students) so that a sense of community within the school is possible. Ernest Boyer's introductory notation to the "Basic School" sounds just right: "If all children are to be ready for school, surely all schools must be ready for the children."[8]

To meet the educational challenges that are upon us now and that will reach major proportions in the 21st century, we need to take seriously the sensibleness about education reform that is evident in the statements and proposals from such commentators as Smith, Kagan, and Boyer. The task before us is neither insurmountable nor obscure. Our public school system is alive and vital. As citizens, we need to turn *to* our public schools, not against them. The public school system needs complementary support mechanisms: 1) a strong, universal preschool policy of support for all children; 2) school-linked programs with social, medical, and welfare agencies that will serve children and youth; 3) resources to provide extended educational programs for children in need; and 4) physical facilities and staff sufficient to create smaller, caring centers of learning for students. Perhaps most of all, the public schools need a reaffirmation by the citizens of the viability of the American common school.

Do I think this will happen? No, I do not. I believe that we will continue to tinker with these problems by establishing special schools that offer examples of success. I see no reason not to concur with Professor Maital's assessment that we are a rich country that acts as if it cannot take care of its poor. Current national and state policy initiatives are designed to make us feel more comfortable about this posture by blaming the poor for their condition of poverty.

Do I think that the concept of the common school will survive as the driving force in American education policy? No, I do not. I believe that an alternative school system, supported substantially by public funds, will be available within the next decade. This change will not occur solely as a result of states adopting voucher plans. More subtly, school systems will be drawn into charter schools, test schools, magnet schools, and contracts with private service providers — a variety of adaptations that will offer ways out of "ordinary" public schools for a significant percentage of the school population. Through entry and retention policies, these schools will be able to avoid learners who are confronting the most difficult financial, family, personal, and educational problems. The beginning years of the 21st century will see a further bifurcation of the rich and the poor at an earlier stage in their lives than is now the case. At some point, I anticipate that the American citizenry will be forced to re-examine its commitment to education for all children and youth in the midst of fierce social strife.

I do not think this picture of education in the 21st century is inevitable, merely likely. Predictions should reflect current conditions. The following trends are gaining strength:

- Increased interest in legislation that authorizes the privatization of schools through vouchers.
- Unremitting attacks on the efficacy of American public schools.
- Acceptance of sharp and distinct classes of citizenry based on wealth.
- Assumption that the public schools already are richly supported and would only waste additional funds.
- Acceptance of the argument that there is insufficient tax leeway to remedy the "problems" of the poor and indigent, in or outside school.

The counterforces to these trends are too divided and too weak to be effective. Educators are capitulating to solutions that ultimately will serve only a portion of the current students in school. Instead of attending to the existing conditions of unwieldy bureaucratization, excessive school and class sizes, underpaid and overburdened teachers, shabby school facilities, and instances of gross under-performance, state policy makers are adopting solutions that avoid confronting the problems. Any policy is considered fair game if it is relatively inexpensive and is focused on the inadequacies of local school officials. Many of these solutions affirm the policy position of those who would give up on the common school by demonstrating that we can operate some effective special schools but we cannot operate an effective school system for all students.

No one should tolerate the failure of public schools to serve *all* students. No one should accept a "solution" that abandons the best for all children in exchange for excellent education for only some children and youth.

Before the millennium, supporters of the common school will be faced with a struggle that they undoubtedly will lose but that is well worth the fight. The public treasury should cover the common entitlement of humankind to education as the basis for responsible citizenship. Some may choose other routes for idiosyncratic reasons motivated by religion, privilege, gender, or ethnicity. Such choices should be allowed by a democratic society but not supported by public taxes. The argument that privatization is no more than the extension of enrollment in private schools to the poor is duplicitous. The academies of the rich will never be open to the disadvantaged, but the common school of the masses can and should be raised to the dream of universal and outstanding education for all.

## Notes

1. Lawrence A. Cremin, *The Genius of American Education* (New York: Random House, 1965), p. 1.
2. "Rallying to Education," *The Nation*, 17 April 1995, p. 1.
3. Myron B. Gubitz, "The Prophet and the Cowboy," *Swiss Review of World Affairs* 2 (February 1995): 5.
4. Children's Defense Fund, *The State of America's Children Yearbook 1994* (Washington, D.C., 1994), p. 2.
5. Frank Smith, "Let's Declare Education a Disaster and Get on with Our Lives," *Phi Delta Kappan* 76 (April 1995): 585.
6. Ibid., p. 596.
7. Sharon L. Kagan, "Normalizing Preschool Education," in *Changing Populations/Changing Schools, Part 2*, edited by Erwin Flaxman and Harry Passow (Chicago: National Society for the Study of Education, University of Chicago Press, 1995), pp. 98-99.
8. Laura Miller, "Boyer Unveils Blueprint for 'Basic School'," *Education Week*, 12 April 1995, p. 12.

# REFLECTIONS OF
# AN URBAN EDUCATOR

## by Jack Kosoy

*Jack Kosoy served as the international president of Phi Delta Kappa from 1991 until 1993. He is an administrator at the Abram Friedman Occupational Center, a vocational school in downtown Los Angeles, California. Jack holds a bachelor's degree from Macalester College in St. Paul, Minnesota, and a master's degree from California State University at Northridge. He has received numerous honors throughout his 35-year career, including being named Teacher of the Year in the Los Angeles School District.*

Let's start with a perspective:

When the verdict came down in the first trial of the policemen who beat up Rodney King, we climbed up to the roof of our Los Angeles school and watched. Building after building around us went up like a roman candle, and the steady din of the crowd and the smell of smoke were punctuated by the staccato of pistol fire. When the smoke cleared and the dust settled, all the buildings in sight were heavily damaged or looted or flattened, except ours. Oh, there were a few stray bullet holes in some of the windows; but frankly, we don't have that many windows.

None of the schools were attacked, nor were any of the people associated with the schools. Like the locally owned businesses, the churches, and the homes of the residents, we are a part of the community. We're staying.

It is from this perspective that I suggest that in spite of the messages of social doomsayers and political apocalyptics, our public education institutions are doing a better job of educating the population now than they have ever done in the past. I believe that the United States, with our system of mandatory education to a certain level of public schooling available to all, is home to the most broadly and deeply educated populace in the world's history. Few studies and statistics are available to back this up, but a look at the unfavorable skew in the statistics that do surface may be sufficient. Most major industrial countries report higher average scores than ours on standardized tests, but every major industrialized country except ours limits access to secondary and higher education — and thus to the pool of test scores — to students who first make it past severe cuts all along the educational process. Still, American scores, while not the highest in the world, are eminently competitive. We provide educational opportunities to everyone in our polyglot culture, not just to an elite few.

Here is a statistic that both suggests our education system is working as we planned it to work and reinforces the meaninglessness of comparing American achievement test scores to scores from countries whose education systems are exclusionary: Forty years ago, in 1955, 50% of students who entered the ninth grade would not complete high school and graduate. Today, better than four out of five ninth-graders will graduate four years later. Today, on the far side of budget cuts that have hurt many genuinely effective programs and under the threatening knife of more cuts to come, the holding power of teachers in the public schools has never been better. Why? I submit that it is because of dedication, caring, and commitment on the part of those people whom the field of public education still attracts, people who spend their lives trying in a very personal way to make a difference in the lives of those who walk through a classroom door.

Are we in fact at risk, as the studies say, of losing our competitive edge on the worldwide stage? Certainly. However, as public education comes under greater attack, I believe that we are at greater risk of becoming another elitist society like those with whom we are competing, of becoming something other than the society we set out to be. In America everyone gets a turn at bat; everyone has equal rights under the law; everyone has access to public education through high school and vocational school. In America we believe in equality of opportunity, and more.

In America we believe in redemption.

I serve a school called the Abram Friedman Occupational Center, a vocational school primarily for young adults in downtown Los Angeles. Our students are people who have genuine practical problems — problems not related to their personal psychologies or inherent anxieties, but rather problems that confront them moment to moment both in and outside the school setting. They have drug dealers on the stoops of their homes; firearms in the cars driving by on the streets; people eager to crawl in from a fire escape if they have the bad judgment to leave a window open on a sweltering Southern California day; pressure to accept and even join in with organized crime in the course of their daily lives and work. Our students are generally people who have had a shot at education and missed out, tripped up, or taken a fall somewhere in the process. They come through our doors looking for redemption.

People growing up in a setting where survival is a grave, immediate concern learn to have few expectations for themselves. Nowhere, even in America, is there equality of opportunity with regard to where or into what family a person is born. Our students come to us when they have exhausted all their other options, and we become a means to survival. By the time our students reach us, they've eliminated most of their more obvious options. Drug dealing either didn't work out or their innate character rejected it out of hand. Gang life was a washout or they repudiated it. Peaceful coexistence with neighborhood tumult proved impossible. What was left was simply to get out, and the way out that occurred to them was through schooling and skill and determination.

Our students come to us with minimal expectations. Perhaps, for some of them, it is just a new way to spend the day. What we try to do — and, in most cases, manage to do — is first demonstrate to them that we believe we can offer them a measure of trust. In return we find that they summon up inner resources of which they previously were unaware.

It is my belief, and the foundation on which I base the management decisions for the institution that I administer, that the key to success in public education is commitment on the part of teachers. Of course, we seek out educators with a particular feel for the community and its needs, but our school is not one of the plum assignments in the sprawling Los Angeles Unified School District. So, rather than starting a teacher search with a number of prerequisites, we start it with a number of assumptions that, maybe just because we believe them, turn out to be warranted:

- The inner city may be the most difficult, but it is certainly the most rewarding environment in which an educator can work.
- Educators who personally strive to make a difference will succeed through the work they do.
- Educators as a class of people are uniformly more dedicated and committed to their mission than any other quarter gives them credit for.
- Educators' personal values — no matter how ignored or maligned, even by the institutions they try to serve — must be

91

reinforced by those with whom they work every bit as much as do their students' aspirations.

- There is no greater source of hope in this or any society than that provided to the student, the community, and the generations to come by a committed teacher.

That's the point at which we start. We do not start there because it is the easiest or the most difficult place to start. We start there because we have found that these assumptions simply provide us with the only firm ground we can find.

Some time ago, Tracy Kidder wrote a book called *The Soul of a New Machine*, in which he explained the "mushroom theory" of management. The way the managers of the growing high-tech corporations of the 1980s oversaw their young technocrats was similar to the best way we have found to let teachers work in the current sociopolitical climate. Kidder suggested that, like the grower of mushrooms, a smart manager of young talent needs to "keep them in the dark, feed them [garbage] and watch them grow." We just try to feed our people a little better than they do in the software business.

Other than the clergy, public education is virtually the last field people enter because they think that by doing so they can do some good in the world. The most important contribution a teacher makes comes not from having knowledge or even from sharing knowledge. It comes from the ability to communicate on a human level with another human being; from the ability inherent in every person capable of making a career decision based on the collective good to touch the soul of another person. Our teachers — the best of them, both in our inner-city schools and elsewhere — can teach without a word, without a book, without a cross glare. Education is not about information; it is about personal resources. As Lord Halifax wrote more than 300 years ago, "Education is what remains when we have forgotten all that we have been taught."

Politics is one of the other fields that is supposed to attract people because they think they can do some good but that more often seems to attract people for all the worst reasons. An old saying holds that politics is the art of the possible.

Education is the art of making things possible.

This week, at our school, we had a number of incidents that might make a lesser person than an educator look elsewhere for a place to spend his or her time. When a gang of thugs empty out of a truck on our premises and beat a student to the point of hospitalization for wearing the wrong colors, you have to wonder whether you're reaching anyone. Then on the same day, a student, who a year earlier walked in for the first time with a sullen face and a chip the size of Dubuque on his shoulder, comes to you and says, "Thank you for making it possible for me to live."

Educators must have a vision of what can be, and must set aside what might mess it up. Because I am an educator, I will continue to overcome; I will always have that vision, because without it there is no direction. One of the sources of pride for me as an urban educator comes from the knowledge that most educators have a vision of what can be.

I once had a student named Eddie, who came into a junior high school where I taught with a look on his face and a chip on his shoulder like the ones I still see students lugging through my doors. He wore that chip and that look like articles of clothing; he worked on them as hard as he worked on his hair before he went out on the prowl. He was a character, and I watched him. I noticed he liked to play ping-pong. I noticed he was pretty good at it. But I was better.

When he had been around for a while, lugging around that chip and all, I challenged him to a game. He thought it was a chance for a little boost in his self-esteem. It would be, but not the way he imagined. I beat him three games in a row, and I was waiting for him to throw down his paddle and stalk off steaming. I didn't goad him — other than by beating him, of course — but he did it. I chased after him.

"Hey, try it once more," I urged Eddie.

He thought I was getting a charge out of beating him, and he spit a string of epithets at me that would have made a Dodge City barmaid blush.

"Yeah, you're right," I told him. "I like beating the kid with the chip on his shoulder. Come on, I'll do it again." And he did play me again. I knew he would.

He beat me. Not by much, but he did. Probably I eased up this time and lost my edge, but he really did work harder for it.

"So listen, Eddie," I said, interrupting his crowing. "Doesn't it feel better to leave the room a winner than a loser?"

"I don't know, man, you tell me how it feels," he continued crowing.

"So what are you going to do with school?" I asked him. "Will you leave here a winner or a loser?"

What he said to that was something like, "Whuh?" but I'm probably not spelling it right.

I made a deal with him. I told him that if he worked as hard every day as he did to win that game, he could have a report card by the end of that year with no grade lower than a C. "What for?" he wanted to know. I told him that it feels better to be a winner than a loser — or hadn't he noticed?

Eddie managed to finish that semester with the report card I had described to him, and he crowed as loudly — and ungraciously, for that matter — as he had when he won that fourth ping-pong game. Watching a kid begin to get good grades is like watching a nine-year-old figure out how to hit a baseball. Once it clicks in, once he gets the hang of it, it just never goes away. Eddie ended his career at our junior high with a straight-A report card and performed just as admirably in high school.

Good story? It isn't over yet.

I've been on the road the past few years, speaking to a lot of education groups around the country. One day 15 years or so after the year with Eddie, I was making a presentation at the University of Southern California County Medical Center for doctors and nurses on reaching their patients on a human level. I walked into a little auditorium on the hospital grounds and there was Eddie — my Eddie, in a suit and tie so conservative he might have been on his way to address the Orange County Rotary Club on debentures.

"What are you doing here?" I wanted to know.

Eddie was administrator of the pediatric pavilion at this major medical institution, with a Ph.D. in hospital management and the most beautiful family I had seen in a long time.

It happens.

It doesn't happen every day. It doesn't always happen soon enough for most of us ever to realize it. It doesn't happen to every life that you touch. But it happens.

For the fact that it happens at all, it is worth having come this way.

# FOR THE LOVE OF LEARNING

## by Arliss L. Roaden

*Arliss L. Roaden is executive director emeritus of the Tennessee Higher Education Commission, having retired in 1995 after 10 years with the commission. He began his career as an elementary teacher in Whitley County, Kentucky, and held a number of positions in schools, colleges, and universities. Arliss served for 11 years as president of Tennessee Technological University in Cookeville before joining the commission. He is a member of the Board of Governors of the Phi Delta Kappa Educational Foundation.*

Learning is unlike any other activity in which we engage. Much of our lives is based on supply and demand. There is a limited amount of money to spend and a finite supply of energy and natural resources, and there never is enough time to do the things we want to do. But learning isn't like that. Supply and demand is not applicable. Learning has no boundaries — no beginning, no ending; the supply of knowledge is unlimited; and the storehouse of the mind is never completely filled.

*Learning Begins Early.* Learning begins early, perhaps before birth. John Dewey advised an expectant mother that she was already late in beginning the education of her unborn child. Perhaps that advice challenges the imagination, but think of the miracle of what a child learns before the age of two — how to talk, walk, care for himself or herself, the basics of numbers and the notion of reading, how to identify objects, and how to share and cooperate with others. Sadly, we know the other side, the negative effects on learning when a pregnant mother uses alcohol or drugs or does not eat a nutritious diet.

The research literature conclusively documents the advantages of introducing books to children and reading to them at a very early age, in fact, soon after birth. And Head Start is one government-sponsored program about which scholars agree on its long-term benefits.

*Learning in the Long Haul.* On the other end of the spectrum of life, learning can be a joy forever. There are many examples of elderly people whose thirst for learning is never quenched. I shall cite two examples, both professional friends, now deceased, whom I respected and admired. My memory of George Reavis and Edgar Dale is still fresh.

Dr. George Reavis retired as an educator and later retired as senior editor of World Books and still later retired from dairy farming. When he was 70, he learned to speak and read Spanish; when he was 80, he learned to play the organ; when he was 84, he gave all that he had to establish the Phi Delta Kappa Educational Foundation, primarily for the purpose of publishing books on education. He died at age 89; but eleven years later, people from around the world gathered at his North Lewisburg, Ohio, home to celebrate his 100th birthday. It has been said, "He planted trees under whose shade he will never sit." But the rest of us will enjoy sitting there, reading a PDK Educational Foundation book.

Dr. Edgar Dale retired as a university professor when he was 65; but after that, he rarely missed a workday in his office, including a half day on Saturdays. He was known for his inquisitive mind and for incessantly asking questions. On one occasion, while he and I were driving to a board meeting, he asked, "Do you have any power?" Then he lectured me on the importance of power and using it wisely and well.

Dr. Dale died at age 82; but during the last years of his life, although he was stricken with Parkinson's disease, he kept on studying, researching, and writing. During the last months of his life, he published four volumes. He once said, "One should not probe the future with too short a stick; excellence takes time."

My high school civics teacher, while lecturing on the importance of learning history, was interrupted by one of the students with the question, "Why do we have to learn this? You can't take it with you."

The teacher responded, "I'm not as certain about that as you apparently are."

That classroom exchange has stuck with me over the years. I'm not so certain about that either. Knowledge and wisdom have a durability that transcends generations and perhaps even life and death. My graduate school professor, years later, said, "Walking the streets of gold will soon become boring if everyone has a blank mind, void of inquisitiveness and imagination — a thirst for learning."

Dr. Betty Siegal, president of Kenesaw College in Georgia, tells of the aging of the college student body that has become typical across the country, as more and more parents and grandparents are returning to college. On graduation day, at Kenesaw College, an octogenarian won the award for being the best history student. The younger students complained, "That's not fair; he lived it."

*Knowledge Is Unlimited.* Unlike the limited supply of money, natural resources, and time, the supply of knowledge is limitless. After graduating from college, spending time in the military service, and witnessing the birth of our two daughters, I was in graduate school. We were visiting one weekend with my family. My grandmother, who was not known for her diplomacy, asked, "What are you doing now?" I responded that I was still in school.

She asked, "Ain't you learned everything there is to know?"

I was reminded of the farmer who, when asked if he had lived all of his life on the same farm, responded, "Not yit."

There is an ever-flowing fountain of knowledge — water, water everywhere — and every drop is to drink. Although we can never consume all of it, we should accept the challenge and keep trying.

*The Mind Is Never Completely Full.* Just as the well of knowledge has no bottom, the mind, the vessel that God gave us to receive knowledge, is never completely filled. There is always room for more. Think of it: a limitless capacity to learn more and more and more!

Abraham Lincoln said, "I don't think much of a man who doesn't know more today than he did yesterday." Abraham Lincoln also was not impressed with artificial time limits. He is credited with the story of a young man who observed a farmer with a shoat in his arms. The farmer was allowing it to eat apples from the apple tree. The young man commented, "Why don't you put the shoat down, shake the apple tree, and let him eat apples off the ground. Look how much time you would save."

The farmer responded, "Young man, time don't mean nothing to a hog."

*The Joy of Learning.* Learning something new is exciting. The four most important words for the learner are: "I didn't know that." Everybody likes to feel special. The way to be special is to experience the ecstasy of learning things no one else knows. If our learning consists only of picking up facts discovered by others, there are technological vacuum cleaners in education that can do that for us better and faster. Philosopher-scientist F.S.C. Northrup said, "The process of science (learning), the running and the checking, can be done by me and me alone; it's as personal as my toothache."

From my oversight role for Tennessee's public colleges and universities, we addressed the challenge of lifting the level of academic quality by establishing on each campus at least one Center of Excellence. Thus each campus has at least one program that is competitive with the best in the world. These centers created pride, and excellence became contagious. So it is with you and me; if we have at least one Center for Excellence in what we know, it rapidly spreads throughout our entire being.

Learning something new every day is more to be prized than those joys described in Homer's great line: "Dear to us ever is the banquet, and the harp, and the dance, and changes in raiment, and the warm bath, and love, and sleep." Learning is better than all of those. Learning soothes the ruffled spirit, heals the frayed nerves, and transforms boredom into excitement. Learning is more refreshing than viewing a sunrise or a sunset, more cleansing than a Saturday night bath.

Regrettably, not everyone drinks deeply from those Empyrean springs of knowledge. Some only gargle. They likely never got started at learning; and their years of schooling were spent in getting through school, rather than basking in learning. Beyond college, on the job, we encounter some folk who apparently took early retirement and forgot to tell anyone. Pope John XXIII, when asked, "How many people work in the Vatican?" responded, "About half of them." My pastor told the story of the deacon who died in church. They called for a physician to check out all of the deacons to find out which one died.

What a waste of life to be among those who retire early from learning. Remember, learning has no beginning and no ending; the storehouse of knowledge is never empty; and our capacity to learn has no boundaries.

*Learning Is Not Confined to Book-Learning.* Book learning is important, but it is not the sole source of learning. Jesse Stuart wrote: "My hills have given me bread; they have put a song in my heart to sing; they have made my brain thirst for knowledge so much that I went beyond my own dark hills to get book knowledge. But I got an earthly degree at home from my own dark soil. I got a degree about birds, cornfields, trees, wild flowers, log shacks, my own people, valleys, and rivers, and mists of the valleys."

*Learning Is Both Theoretical and Practical.* We often hear students say, "I don't need to learn that; I'll never use it." Nonsense! We use everything in living. In the comic strip, "Beetle Bailey," soldiers Beetle and Zero were standing by the roadside in Camp Swampy when a loaded garbage truck passed. Killer and Plato were sitting in the middle of the garbage. Beetle said, "Look at Killer and Plato. Did you know that Plato has a college degree in philosophy?" Zero responded, "If he has a college degree in philosophy, what's he doing on that garbage truck?" And Beetle said, "Let's face it, where would you need a college degree in philosophy more?"

Today's school leaders are seeking a curriculum that arises from and teaches solid values that allow for successful interchanges between the theoretical and the practical. For many educators and others, this concern translates into learning to practice civility, the art of loving your neighbor as yourself.

More than 20 years ago, Edgar Dale wrote an unpublished paper on civility. He gave me the original copy. Edgar first read these words at a meeting of the Ohio State University Chapter of Phi Delta Kappa:

> Today we are in a period of self-examination. There is a hunger for kindness, gentleness, fair play. Let's look more closely at our values — the goals of a decent society.
>
> The men and women whom we admire will put in more than they take out. They are broadly cooperative where others are narrowly competitive. They see life not as a ladder but as a spiraling circle with room enough for everyone to reach a high level. They are "we" centered, not "me" centered. They have bifocal vision — can see both the present and the future. They look to the past lovingly, but not longingly; they have no need for comforting nostalgia. They look forward, not backward. They plant trees under whose shade they'll never sit. To quote William James, "They spend their life working for something that will outlast them."
>
> They are empathetic — move easily into other people's shoes and let others move into theirs. They have extra-sensory perception. They are mentors for the unloved, and dispossessed, the homeless, the walking wounded. They do not humiliate other people, but patiently and wisely help them learn to respect themselves and others.
>
> They learn how to invest their time, their energy, and money to bring the greatest social and individual returns. They are deeply attached to thinking but not to things. They have had access to the best in learning and are striving to make that available to others. They are not all-wise, but they do have their ignorance well organized. They know what they know and what they don't know.

They do not shrug off violations of trust and justice saying, "Well, that's life."

They have a capacity for indignation. They do tolerate a certain amount of ambiguity but realize that there are decision points when you must say "yes" or "no" and sometimes resoundingly. They believe with Samuel Johnson that everything that enlarges the sphere of human powers, that shows man he can do what he thought he could not do, is valuable. They help people think better of themselves.

When my children were growing up and I corrected them for some misdeed, they often would say, "Daddy, nobody is perfect." I tried to teach them that perfection is more in the pursuit than in the achievement. Someone wrote, "Ideals are like stars for the seafaring man on a desert of sea; you never succeed in touching them with your hand, but you use them as your guide."

Discussion of learning stimulates discussion of teaching. When one reflects on his or her schooling, a few teachers — perhaps only one or two — stand out. Those are the ones who help chart the course of one's life.

Dr. Harold Fawcett, the late professor of mathematics and education at Ohio State University, told me of his early schooling in Canada. He described it as routine and boring until he encountered Miss Mary, his fifth-grade teacher, who stimulated his excitement about the joys of learning. During those days, the students recited Bible verses each morning. One was from Psalms, "Surely goodness and mercy shall follow me all the days of my life." Dr. Fawcett recalled that it was years later when he learned the real words of that psalm. He had thought that he and his fellow students were saying, "Surely good Miss Mary shall follow me all the days of my life." He concluded that good Miss Mary had, indeed, followed him all of his life.

One of my professors, Dr. Orin Graff, influenced my life more than anyone else except for my parents. He taught his students that they could be more than they ever thought they could become. His admonition was that of architect and engineer Horace Barnum, who wrote, "Make no little plans. They have no magic to stir men's souls and probably themselves will never be realized. Make big plans. Aim high in hope and work, remembering that a noble logical diagram, once recorded, will never die, but long after we are gone, will be a living thing, asserting itself with every growing insistence. . . . Let your watchword be order and your beacon beauty."

One day while Professor Graff was lecturing in his philosophy of education class, he was quoting his former professor, Boyd Bode, whose textbook we were using. He mentioned Dr. Bode's death many years earlier. Then his voice broke and he cried. I thought, how strange for a distinguished professor to be so emotionally attached to the memory of his former teacher that he would cry. I must confess that years later when Professor Graff died, I cried too.

Bonds grow between learners and teachers. But there also is an addiction to learning. Learners cannot be deprived of books, art, music, and an association with other learners, who are often likely to be teachers. Recently, I reread Boswell's biography of Samuel Johnson, the incessant learner. Johnson was always seeking the company of one or more scholars with whom he would debate ideas and the merits of the work of other scholars.

Both learning and teaching are processes that become synonymous with products because there is no defined beginning or ending. Alfred North Whitehead advised that, "The process is itself the actuality since we no sooner arrive than we start on a fresh journey." And what an exciting journey it is!

# AN EYE ON THE FUTURE
# IN SOUTH AFRICA

by Neville Robertson

*Neville Robertson formerly headed Phi Delta Kappa's Center for Dissemination of Innovative Programs and now serves PDK Headquarters as a roving troubleshooter, principally overseeing electronic innovations planning and cooperative marketing efforts. Neville's international career has spanned many decades, during which time he has kept his keen eyes on the changes in his birthplace, southern Africa.*

Growing up as a white male student in southern Africa gave me an excellent academic background but taught me very little about the complex society in which I lived. It was not that I did not observe what was going on around me; but, like my fellow students and indeed the white adult population in general, I thought it was how things were meant to be. I certainly did not have any strong motivation or reason to change the order of things. I did not recognize that I was a member of a small, privileged group and that I was enjoying a quality of life that was surpassed only in the United States and in a few selected parts of Europe.

Most of my elementary schooling was in northern Rhodesia (now Zambia), my high school years were spent in southern Rhodesia (now Zimbabwe), and my undergraduate studies and two years of graduate work were completed at Rhodes University in South Africa. In many ways, not surprisingly, this was the most exciting and happiest period of my life. The 13 years I spent in primary and secondary education — to use the British terminology — was a period of absolute joy. The schools I attended were under the control of the respective ministries of education; they were therefore not private schools, but government schools. And our teachers were outstanding, which should not come as a surprise because they were the highest-paid teachers in the British Commonwealth. Of course, this meant that the teachers were recruited from some of the finest schools in Britain, other British colonies, and

South Africa. They were able to take sabbaticals of six months every three years, and we students benefited a great deal from their professional development experiences.

Our school year consisted of 196 days with three vacations, two of three weeks each and one of six weeks. The six years of high school work required me to take eight subjects each year, namely English and English Literature, Mathematics, Physics, Chemistry, French, Latin, History, and Geography. At the end of our eleventh year, we wrote the Cambridge University (Ordinary Level) certificate — this being the school-leaving certificate and probably best described as the equivalent of a high school diploma in the United States. Students going on to college remained at school for an additional two years and then wrote the Cambridge University (Higher Level) certificate for college entrance requirements. Both examinations were graded in Britain.

More important than any of the details I have given above was the excellent rapport between teachers and students, both in the classroom and in extracurricular activities. I attribute this to a number of factors: the high regard that teachers enjoyed in their respective communities, the high level of interest and support that parents gave their children, and the close friendships that developed between teachers and parents. My own experience as a teacher in Rhodesia for 15 years confirmed the impressions that I observed as a high school student. During my stay in South Africa, which also included an eight-year period as a human resources researcher, I visited a number of schools and universities. Although the Zimbabwean (Rhodesian) and South African education systems differed in many ways (for example, 13 years of schooling in Zimbabwe versus 12 years in South Africa), they also shared a number of similarities, particularly with respect to teacher-student-parent relationships.

My original purpose in writing this essay was to compare the approaches to education and training in these two countries: Zimbabwe and South Africa. However, two factors led me alter direction and to focus on South Africa: 1) the current international interest in South Africa, and 2) the difficulty of finding accurate and reliable data about Zimbabwe.

I have sketched my own school experience as a backdrop in order to contrast the education received by students of other races less fortunate than I. Although some improvements have been made in the education system over the years, the situation for many students has not changed significantly. This is having — and will continue to have — a tremendous bearing on the future of post-independence South Africa. It also has definite implications for how other nations will decide whether or not to invest in South Africa.

Certainly, South Africa is a country blessed with an abundance of natural resources, which has resulted in many optimistic predictions that South Africa will be one of the economic wonders of the 21st century. The development of its human resources through education and training will be a key ingredient. The purpose of this essay is to analyze the problems and prospects of this beautiful but still divided country.

## Pre-Independence South Africa

South Africa under the apartheid regime was in many ways no different from any country that practiced discrimination against certain groups of people within its borders. However, it did have a unique feature — discrimination was the law of the land. *De jure* discrimination rather than *de facto* discrimination was the order of the day. Either way, the violation of human rights could be equally severe; but significant change was made more difficult where legislation had to be repealed through a drawn-out process.

South Africa under apartheid was held together by numerous acts of parliament. Among these were the notorious Land Acts, which restricted 87% of the African (Black) population to 13% of the land; the Group Areas Act, which prescribed where the Africans working in White areas could live on a temporary basis; the Population Registration Act, which classified the race of all inhabitants by means of identity cards that could determine the fate of any individual for the rest of his or her life; and the Job Reservation Act, which fixed the limits of jobs open to people of color. Although these and many other acts were later repealed, particularly during the 1990s, real movement in this direction began only when it became obvious that major constitutional change was inevitable. The effect on the various peoples of South Africa by these acts can be easily gauged when it is recognized that with a population of approximately 40 million, Africans make up 76%, Asians 3%, Colored (mixed races) 9%, and Whites 13% of the total.[1]

Jose Ortego y Gassett, the Spanish philosopher, is reputed to have said, "Education is a mirror of the society that it serves." Education under apartheid came very close to that description, which can be illustrated by a statement released on 17 June 1954 by the then-Minister of Bantu (Black) Education, Hendrik Verwoerd. He said:

> My department's policy is that education should stand with both feet in the reserves [lands reserved for Africans] and have its roots in

the spirit and being of Bantu society. There Bantu education must be able to give itself complete expression and there it will be called upon to perform its real service. The Bantu must be guided to serve his own community in all respects. There is no place for him in the European community above the level of certain forms of labor. Within his own community, however, all doors are open. For that reason it is of no avail for him to receive a training which has as its aim absorption in the European community, where he cannot be absorbed. Until now he has been subjected to a school system which drew him away from his own community and misled him by showing him the green pastures of European society in which he was not allowed to graze. This attitude is not only uneconomic because money is spent for education that has no specified aim, but is also dishonest to continue it. The effect on the Bantu community we find is the much discussed frustration of educated natives who can find no employment which is acceptable to them. It is abundantly clear that unplanned education creates many problems, disrupting the community life of the Bantu and endangering the community life of the European.

This statement became the blueprint for education in South Africa for the next 40 years. Verwoerd later became prime minister of South Africa until his death in 1966. He will always be known as the "Architect of Apartheid." Although in many ways he was sincere in his belief that the culture of a society should be of paramount importance, it is difficult to justify apartheid on these grounds. Apartheid should be seen for what it was: a rationalization for discriminating against the majority of the inhabitants of South Africa. Even the Dutch Reformed Church, the largest religion practiced in the country, for many years drew on texts from the Bible to support its attitude toward people of color by regarding them as "the hewers of wood and the drawers of water."

The outcome was that education in South Africa was segregated by law into four main categories: African education, Colored education, Asian education, and White education. The medium of instruction was determined by the mother tongue of the students, and schools were established to meet this need. White Afrikaans-speaking students attended their own schools, as did English-speaking students. Each received instruction in all subjects in their mother tongue only for the first four years, and then learned the other official language (English or Afrikaans) as a compulsory subject for the next eight years. Asian and Colored schools followed the same format as did White schools.

By contrast, African students were taught in their mother tongue —
as many as 11 such languages have been identified — through the first
seven years, and only then were required to add English and Afrikaans
as subjects. Therefore, it is not surprising that many of them believed
that they were being excluded from developing proficiency in the two
official languages in order to ensure that they would be at a disadvantage relative to the other three groups.

However, the greatest criticism must be reserved for school funding,
which fostered wide discrepancies among the different racial groups.
This problem is illustrated in Table 1.

**Table 1. Per capita expenditure in rand on primary and secondary students
by race.[2]**

| Year | African | Colored | Asian | White |
|---|---|---|---|---|
| 1969/70 | 25 | 94 | 124 | 461 |
| 1979/80 | 91 | 234 | 389 | 1,169 |
| 1989/90 | 930 | 1,983 | 2,659 | 3,739 |

According to the data in Table 1, White students had a significant
advantage over other racial groups. Although the ratio of per capita
expenditures for White students to African students dropped — from
18 to 1 in 1969/70 to 4 to 1 in 1989/90 — it still left the African student at a distinct disadvantage.

I worked with the late Denis Etheridge, who was director of the
Anglo American Corporation, on a number of projects. Etheridge listed
the consequences for African students of the lower funding as: overcrowded classrooms (despite double sessions), a higher teacher-student
ratio (1 to 46 for Africans as against 1 to 19 for Whites), and inadequate
furniture, equipment, laboratories, libraries, sports, and sport equipment. Teaching science without laboratories was like coaching football
without a ball.

It also meant inadequately trained, overworked, and poorly paid
teachers for African schools. Even at the beginning of 1990, 15% of
African teachers did not hold a professional certificate, 26% had graduated from high school but were not professionally certificated, 36%
had a high school diploma and six months of professional training, 22%
held a high school diploma and had received three years of professional training, and only 5% had graduated from college.

In contrast, almost without exception, White teachers were professionally qualified. It was therefore most unfortunate that in the period

1987 through 1990, when African enrollment at teacher training colleges increased by 51%, there was a decline of 30% of White students attending teacher training colleges. The situation was made even more bleak by the fact that most African children came from poor homes, financially and culturally, overcrowded houses in which doing homework presented major difficulties. And they lived in areas that often were beset with violence. It was a minor miracle that so many of them did well at school.

I have highlighted the problems facing the African student relative to the White student. But it must be emphasized that Colored and Asian students also suffered different degrees of educational neglect. In March 1991, Brian Stewart, managing director of the Kwazulu Training Trust, estimated that 78% of Africans, 55% of Coloreds, 23% of Asians, and 2% of Whites were illiterate.[3] Probably the most disturbing statistic was that 71% of African students had dropped out of school by the end of their seventh year. Similarly, of the 253,623 African students enrolled in the final year of high school, only 37% received a high school diploma and only 8% obtained a matriculation exemption that would allow them to enter the universities. Figures for the other three racial groups were: Colored (79%, 20%), Asian (95%, 45%), and White (96%, 41%). Enrollment at Technical Colleges for courses exceeding three or more years was only 613, of which 581 were Whites and 32 were Coloreds. No Africans and Asians were enrolled in these courses.

A more encouraging picture emerges when looking at the increased numbers of students attending universities during the decade of the 1980s. Whereas African students numbered 10,681 in 1980, 10 years later that figure had changed to 104,130, almost a ten-fold increase. Over the same period, Coloreds increased by only 1,558 from 16,088 to 17,647. Asians, on the other hand, had moved from 11,679 to 18,827; and White students increased from 83,353 to 153,035.[4]

The economic implications of these statistics are important. Of the economically active population in 1990, 7.4 million were Africans, 1.2 million were Coloreds, 350,000 were Asians, and two million were Whites. However, the employment distribution may be more revealing. Statistics from five years earlier show that in 1985, Africans occupied only 4% of high-level positions (excluding nursing and teaching), Coloreds 2.5%, Asians 2.8%, and Whites 90.7%. The discrepancy was less marked at the middle-level positions, where Africans occupied 23% of the positions; Coloreds 11.5%: Asians 5.5%; and Whites 59.9%. In semi-skilled and unskilled positions, Africans provided 79%; Colored 12.6%; Asians 2.9%; and Whites 5.4% In 1990, of the 126,523 persons who registered as unemployed, 76,235 were Africans, 22,448 were Coloreds, 8,000 were Asians, and 19,840 were Whites.[5]

A 1993 World Bank report estimated that South African Whites had a per capita income that was 9.5 times higher than Africans, 4.5 times higher than Coloreds, and 3 times higher than people classified as Asians under the apartheid system.[6] It goes without saying that access to education, housing, employment opportunities, and wealth generation did, and still do, heavily favor the Whites.

The preceding discussion presents a pessimistic picture for the future of South Africa. Thus a key question must be, given this view, how can South Africa achieve the great potential that many observers believe it has?

## The New South Africa: Beliefs and Strategies for Development

Before discussing beliefs and strategies, it is useful to recognize that on Independence Day, 19 April 1994, South Africa had been out of the mainstream of global events for nearly a decade because of international sanctions. It returned to a much-changed economic world characterized by single-minded participants with unforgiving rules. No longer can South Africa rely on its former friends to smooth its way in this new environment, because those friends have now become competitors. Post-independence South Africa must therefore make its own way and move forward taking account of its own national interests, but at the same time developing a circumspect understanding of the vagaries of the global scene.[7]

Nelson Mandela, just prior to becoming president, spelled out his following beliefs with respect to future foreign policy:

- that issues of human rights are central to international relations and an understanding that they extend beyond the political, embracing the economic, social and environmental;
- that just and lasting solutions to the problems of humankind can only come through the promotion of democracy worldwide;
- that consideration of justice and respect for international law should guide the relations between nations;
- that peace is the goal for which all nations should strive, and where this breaks down, internationally agreed and nonviolent mechanisms, including effective arms-control regimes, must be employed;
- that the concerns and interests of the continent of Africa should be reflected in our foreign-policy choices;

- that economic development depends on growing regional and international cooperation in an interdependent world.[8]

This set of beliefs represents a 180-degree turn from those implemented under the apartheid system from 1948 until independence.

Although I previously described education and training as the key ingredients in the future development of the new South Africa, a number of other factors also will play important roles. These factors include political stability, wealth distribution, homogeneity of population, labor market stability, ability to service external debt, inflation trends, imports and exports, monetary and fiscal discipline, and job creation. This list is by no means exhaustive, but it does illustrate the comprehensive approach that is required if the country is to achieve its objectives.

One of the major shortcomings of the colonial powers in Africa and elsewhere was their single-minded approach to education. Education became an end in itself, and no consideration was given to the kinds of jobs that would be waiting for the students when they had completed their studies. Many students became disillusioned because their expectations were not met; as a result, various social problems followed.

Thus the critical area in the development of the new South Africa is going to be the development of its human resources. There are major discrepancies both in numbers and quality for the skills required to make South Africa a viable player, both on the world scene and at home. Therefore the nation's leaders cannot tackle education and training as a sole focus. However important this area is, the country must tackle its problems on a broad front; otherwise it will not succeed. For example, the rural areas face massive problems of overpopulation, poverty, lack of housing, and disease. Unless these are attended to, education and training will have little or no meaning. Following are some of the strategies that will make up an action plan, both for short term and for the long term.

Probably the most pressing matter is housing. The majority of Africans do not have adequate shelter. Seldom do they have piped water, electricity, or sewage systems in their homes. Efforts are being made to rectify these inadequacies, but this is a mammoth task and will take years to complete.

Health care falls into the same category. Not only are infant mortality rates extremely high, but life expectancy, particularly in rural areas, is often less than 40 years. Doctors, nurses, and clinic personnel are in short supply. Spectacular improvements are possible when qualified persons and adequate facilities are in place. But, unfortunately, this objective also must be seen in the long term.

110

Poor agricultural methods mean that food supplies often fall below the levels required to meet the needs of an expanding population. Fortunately, some progress has been made because of the training in the schools of agriculture for all races. One of the major mistakes in the past was to train African farmers but not provide them with the necessary venture capital to reap the benefits of the their new skills. Reasonably good and quick returns are possible, provided adequate funding is made available. Nevertheless, farmers from all four racial groups still face the possibility of droughts, some of which may go on for years.

South Africa also needs to expand its trading efforts. Until recently, South Africa's exports to the southern African region (Lesotho, Swaziland, Botswana, Namibia, Zimbabwe, Mozambique, Malawi, and Zambia) exceeded imports from that region by more than five to one. Not only would a closer balance of trade benefit all countries, but South Africa would no longer be in a dominating role. By creating more equal partners, South Africa, as an importer, would be strengthening its own marketplace and, at the same time, providing incentives to other countries to develop their own resources and provide a strong base for a regional trading unit. This move also would fulfill Mandela's belief that he should support both regional and national trade in Africa as his first priority — before giving consideration to other international trading links. However, by strengthening his African ties, he would be enhancing the likelihood of trading links with non-African countries as well.[9]

In the short term, there will be a need to create jobs in the urban and rural areas; assist small business ventures, particularly for African entrepreneurs; improve basic services, such as access to water supplies, electrification, and water-borne sewage; and restructure social security programs for the very poor, the disabled, and the aged.[10]

As for education, the first step in reform came into effect on 1 January 1995 with the introduction of "ten years free and compulsory education." A beginning was made by enrolling all six-year-olds in first grade. However, enforcing compulsory education across all grades will not be possible in the short term, because South Africa lacks professionally trained teachers and the facilities to house all of the students. Consequently, the plan is to phase in each age group over a period of years. In the first year, only six-year-olds will be affected. In the second year, compulsory education will extend to all six- and seven-year-olds. And so on.

Another of the main difficulties facing the introduction of compulsory schooling is that parents of African children have not been required to supply birth registration as a precondition for their children's entry into school. Birth registration was not necessary because children were not required to attend school. To overcome this problem, it will be necessary to educate parents as to the requirements for entering school. Many parents may not be able to obtain the necessary documentation because such records are not available.

The government hopes to continue to include more students in the compulsory framework as more school funding becomes available. A major concern has been the fate of students in grades 11 and 12. The intent is to provide state subsidies for a significant number of these students, particularly those from socioeconomically disadvantaged homes. In certain instances, parents may be required to contribute to the cost of schooling at this level. The intent is to ensure that as many as possible of these students will be able to proceed to the matriculation and beyond.[11]

## Foreign Investment

Significant foreign investment is necessary for South Africa to become an international player. Furthermore, this investment will need to come within three to seven years. Current expectations are high among all sections of the South African population, but a sense of impatience is developing among certain militant groups who believe that progress has been too slow. At the same time, there are those among the White community who are unlikely ever to accept the new government and those young Africans who feel that the old guard, including Mandela, are not aggressive enough in providing the changes that they are convinced can be effected in a much shorter time. If the population's expectations are not met in a reasonable length of time, opposition to the new administration is likely to grow and may result in more of the violence that has become commonplace in South Africa. Strong foreign investment in the next few years will be the best counter to the return of the old conditions.

In spite of these currents of potential discontent, there are indicators that investment in the new South Africa may be closer at hand than many South Africa watchers believe. This is because South Africa is receiving promising "risk" ratings for investment. These ratings are a reference for country comparisons and are used by lenders as a benchmark for risk. Typically, these ratings are reviewed annually, or more frequently if something dramatic occurs in the interim. Three of the more prestigious rating services are Moody's, Standard and Poor's, and Nippon Investment Services. Recently, Moody's and Nippon Services both rated South Africa as BBB, which is a medium grade. Although this is the lowest grade for investment, it is not a rejection. Standard and Poor issued a speculative BB rating with a "positive outlook" stamp of approval.

The Centre for Research into Economics and Finance at the London School of Economics believes that these ratings provide a platform for ratings improvement in the medium term. Since the release of these ratings, certain changes in South Africa have occurred that are likely to have a positive effect when new ratings are announced. Such changes include abandonment of the two-tier money system in March 1995 (one of the major impediments to investment in South Africa), privatization of state assets to reduce government debt, the cutting of the public service by 10%, and a 10% reduction in ministerial salaries. (In fact, Mandela cut his own salary by 20%.) Probably the most significant of these changes is the privatization of state assets. Although nationalization was a cornerstone of the African National Congress (ANC) policies in the negotiations leading up to independence, this objective was a red flag as far as industrialized countries were concerned. Privatization could pave the way for more investment than was previously thought likely.[12]

It also is interesting to note that some South Africans already are investing in other countries. The prime example is the South African paper and pulp producer, SAPPI, which recently has acquired S.D. Warren, the world's largest manufacturer of coated, wood-free paper, at a cost of US$1.6 billion. This investment is not only in the United States, but also in Britain, Germany, and the Far East. At the present time, South Africa is bidding for the contract to build the Rooivalk combat helicopter for Britain, which is estimated to be a US$3 billion contract; and the South Africans have an excellent chance of winning that contract. Such efforts as these could well inspire foreign investors to look long and hard at the possibilities that South Africa offers.[13]

### Will the United States Invest in South Africa?

In conclusion, the question must be brought home to the United States. Why should U.S. educators — indeed North American educators — concern themselves with a nation that is half a world away? That question becomes one of how the United States and South Africa are, or might be, linked in an interdependent world economy. And so, ultimately, after eight years of economic sanctions, the question reduces to: Will the United States invest in South Africa?

The short answer is yes. But to answer this question fully, five areas must be considered: 1) companies currently doing business in South

Africa, 2) exchange rates and the two-tier monetary system, 3) housing, 4) cultural exchanges, and 5) worldwide democracy.

*Companies Currently Doing Business in South Africa.* From 1985 through 1993, trade sanctions were imposed on South Africa because of its apartheid policies. Two hundred and nine U.S. companies sold or closed their South African subsidiaries or offices. The number of remaining companies had dropped to 104 by 1991. In July 1991 President Bush lifted the five-year ban on new U.S. investment. By September 1993 another 32 U.S. companies had established themselves in South Africa. Following Nelson Mandela's call for the lifting of world sanctions as preparation for the holding of democratic elections in April 1994, another 30 U.S. companies had been added by October. As of 1 May 1995 the total of U.S. companies doing business in South Africa was 206.[14]

A listing of these companies includes many big names, such as IBM, Microsoft, Coca-Cola, PepsiCo, McDonalds, Johnson and Johnson, Eastman Kodak, Nike, Hyatt International, Minnesota Mining and Manufacturing (3M), and Ford Motor Company. When companies of this stature are prepared to do business in South Africa, they must have confidence in the future.

*Exchange Rates and the Two-Tier Monetary System.* The two-tier system consisted of a financial rand and a commercial rand. The one was for domestic use, the other for foreign investment. The intent was to provide the would-be investor with a number of incentives in South Africa. Unfortunately, if the company decided to discontinue the operation, the investor was penalized by receiving only the lower domestic rate when the company left South Africa. As can be imagined, many a potential investor turned elsewhere. This system was abandoned in March 1995 and replaced by a single rand as the monetary unit. Industrialized countries immediately responded positively, and the change should lead to increased interest in investment.

The current exchange rate of approximately US$0.27 to the rand is very attractive to an investor. However, as South Africa's economy gains momentum, those rates are likely to rise and lose some of their attractiveness.

*Housing.* Housing is one of the most critical needs facing South Africa. It is unlikely that a good standard of permanent housing for all inhabitants, particularly rural Africans, can be accomplished in the short term. Almost certainly there will be a long transition period where good but temporary housing will have to be provided. The U.S. construction industry is well-equipped to deal with these situations. Not only would it benefit the U.S. company, but such an investment would create jobs.

*Cultural Exchange.* South Africans have long ties with the United States through cultural exchanges and through the awarding of scholarships. For example, the School of Business at the University of Cape Town was established by faculty from the Harvard School of Business. These faculty spent extended periods in Cape Town and developed what became the model for all subsequent schools of business at other South African universities. In post-independence South Africa, the opportunity for widening these exchanges is almost limitless. Possible strategies could include using American educators to establish teacher training programs for the unqualified and minimally qualified teachers who currently are responsible for teaching a significant proportion of African and Colored children. With the introduction of compulsory education, the need for professionally trained teachers in the next decade will become tremendous. Similar efforts could be made in health care and agricultural and industrial training. Again, this will not be a one-way strategy. South Africa is both a First World and a Third World country. As such, foreign scholars, educators, business personnel, and other professionals should be enriched by their experiences and carry home with them new perspectives that might be of benefit in their home communities.

*Worldwide Democracy.* Since the days of the spice trade between Europe and the Far East, South Africa has been seen as holding a strategic role in world affairs by virtue of its geographic location. This view continued to be held until the end of World War II. With the advance of technology, this role has all but disappeared. Nevertheless, a new and equally important role has emerged in the democratization of many areas in Africa after a long period of socialist and one-party governments. Southern Africa, and South Africa in particular, has moved in this direction in recent years and promises to be in the forefront of this movement. Mandela, himself, is probably the strongest advocate of worldwide democracy. Thus the increasing ties between the United States and South Africa should provide the foundation for common national interests

The key to the future for South Africa remains the development of its human resources. America can play a positive role if it chooses to do so. That choice would be in our best interest.

115

# References

1. Carole Cooper, Robin Hamilton, and Harry Mashabela, *Race Relations Survey 1991/92* (Johannesburg: South African Institute of Race Relations, 1992), p. 1.
2. Ibid., p. 108.
3. Brian Stewart, cited in the East London *Daily Dispatch*, 2 March 1991.
4. Cooper, Hamilton, and Mashabela, pp. 205-21.
5. Ibid., p. 240.
6. International Bank for Reconstruction and Development, *World Development Report 1994: Infrastructure for Development* (New York: Oxford University Press, World Bank, 1993).
7. Gail Lefwich, "The Hard Work of Being Ordinary," *South Africa: The Journal of Trade, Industry and Investment* (February/March 1995): 5.
8. Nelson Mandela, "South Africa's Future Foreign Policy," *Foreign Affairs* 71 (November/December 1993): 87.
9. Ibid., p. 90.
10. Ibid., p. 94.
11. Republic of South Africa Government Gazette, *White Paper on Education and Training* (Cape Town: Department of Education, 15 March 1995), pp. 73-78.
12. Ciaran Ryan, "The Risk You Take," *South Africa: The Journal of Trade, Industry and Investment* (February/March 1995): 6-10.
13. Ciaran Ryan, "Out of the Woodwork," *South Africa: The Journal of Trade, Industry and Investment* (February/March 1995): 52-55.
14. Investor Responsibility Research Center, South African Review Service, 1350 Connecticut, N.W., Washington, DC 20036-1701, (Personal communication by telephone and fax) 15 May 1995.